CHILDREN IN THE BALANCE

CHILDREN IN THE BALANCE

*Ina Schlesinger
and
Michael D'Amore*

CITATION PRESS

NEW YORK

1971

LIBRARY OF CONGRESS CATALOG CARD NUMBER: 70-152227
STANDARD BOOK NUMBER: 590-09482-3

Designed by Jean Smith Pollack
Cover by June Martin

CONTENTS

CONTENTS

FOREWORD

This country today consists of two separate societies that, as the President's Commission on Violence pointed out, are becoming increasingly polarized. Only in some public schools is a conscious and deliberate attempt being made to bring together and merge into one these two different Americas. Some communities have decided to integrate their schools in disregard of local residential patterns. It is likely that others will follow suit.

Plans of this nature, though well-intentioned, have often been drawn up without true knowledge of the problem involved. When difficulties become apparent, too often they are met with a hostility born of disappointment or are entirely ignored. Relations between the races is one of the basic problems in American society today. Whether or not we decide to integrate our schools, the two worlds will have to learn somehow to live together and deal with each other.

In this book we propose to describe what actually happened, as we saw it, in the schools of White Plains, New York, over a period of five years after the decision to integrate was implemented.

For obvious reasons all names of children have been changed. The views expressed by the authors do not reflect in any way the views or opinions of the White Plains Board of Education, education officials, or any one other than the two individual writers.

Putting children together in one classroom is only a first step; it is desegregation rather than integration. The real work begins only *after* this first step has been taken. In the classroom a teacher is now faced with: the age-old suspicion and distrust of black people; the "monumental hypocrisy" of whites; prejudice, blindness, and ignorance on both sides; two widely different sets of values, attitudes, and needs; and the disparity in academic standards created by the ghetto. All this must be dealt with patiently and realistically if integration is to become a fact.

Both authors worked with the children discussed in this book, one as the classroom teacher, the other as a volunteer. The "I" in the book reflects our joint feelings and experiences. As we discussed each incident that came up in the classroom, we often found that we had to evaluate and reevaluate many times our initial reactions and interpretations. Since we are both from a white middle-class background, we began with the assumption that our standards should be accepted by all. As we shared our experiences, we came to realize the existence of *two* worlds and *two* sets of standards, both with an equal right to our respect. We are now beginning to see race as part of the child's individuality rather than as a factor setting him apart into a different world. Above all, our experiences have taught us that understanding in the classroom can begin only after we learn to *see* each other.

Ina Schlesinger
Michael D'Armore

THE BACKGROUND

White Plains, New York, is a community of about 58,000 people. The county center of Westchester County, it contains many businesses as well as serving as a suburban "bedroom" for commuters who work in New York City. Socially and economically, the population ranges from wealthy, upper middle-class families down to a hard-core poverty group—largely black—who form a pocket of want in the midst of a truly affluent society.

The black population, about 20 per cent of the total, is concentrated in the inner or center city. For the most part, the blacks live either in old slum dwellings (some of which lack even indoor toilet facilities) or in comparatively new "projects." The latter are large apartment-house complexes that house a large number of black families under woefully overcrowded conditions. The housing situation is deteriorating, at this writing, since the city's urban renewal program has torn down many of the old houses without providing new housing facilities in the area.

White Plains has few middle-class black families; those who work in the city live elsewhere. When the urban renewal plan was being worked out, a proposal for building scattered housing, rather than high-rise apartments, to replace the slum dwellings was widely discussed throughout the city. Opposition from the white population was so intense that the plan had to be abandoned. The result is that neighborhood elementary schools in many middle-class neighborhoods remained entirely white.

The White Plains schools enjoy an excellent academic

reputation. The three junior and one senior high schools have always been integrated, as their students have been drawn from the community as a whole. Before 1964, of the eleven elementary schools in the city, five had virtually all-white school populations, while one—Rochambeau school—was becoming increasingly black.

The problem of racial imbalance became the direct concern of the White Plains school board in 1963; in that year the State Commissioner of Education sent out to all school districts a letter dealing with this issue. A racially imbalanced school was defined as one with 50 per cent or more black children. When the black population reached this figure in a school, experience had shown that white families began to move out of the neighborhood, leaving the school to become totally black. It was the consensus of educators at that time that an all-black school tends to have very harmful effects on youngsters attending it. Academic standards and physical facilities in a racially segregated school tend to deteriorate, and the best teachers go elsewhere. The self-image of the black children, moreover, is very materially affected. The Commissioner's letter ended with a request for information on which school districts contained racially imbalanced schools and what the school board planned to do about it.

The letter from Albany served to point up a problem with which the school board in White Plains was becoming increasingly concerned. Rochambeau school was well within the definition of racial imbalance; 62 per cent of its population was black, and the percentage had been steadily increasing as more black people moved into the city. Unrest in neighboring communities had shown clearly that inaction would only aggravate the problem. Fully aware of the problem, the school board had been trying for some time piecemeal measures to alleviate the situation. School attendance areas had been redrawn to provide for more racial balance in the elementary schools. A new elementary school was built to replace one in a predominantly black area; this building was purposely located on the boundary line of two housing districts to draw its students from white and black neighborhoods alike. Finally, when it became necessary to expand the high school, the board decided to build a new one that would serve the entire city, rather than build a second school, which would almost inevitably divide the high school population according to race.

None of these measures, however, could affect the trend in Rochambeau school, and by 1964, it had become clear that more drastic solutions were needed. The board therefore decided to close Rochambeau school and distribute its pupils among the elementary schools throughout the rest of the city. The black elementary school population of White Plains made up 19 per cent of the total enrollment. Based on these figures, the school board ruled that under the new plan no school should have less than 10 per cent or more than 30 per cent black children. Rochambeau school had 500 pupils at the time. If all were to be reassigned, busing would have to be provided for about 300 children.

The board decided to implement this plan in April 1964. Although the decision did not have to be submitted for public approval, the problem remained how to persuade the community, particularly parents (white and black) whose children were personally affected, to accept the plan.

The board decided to introduce the plan first at a meeting of leading officials in service, civic, neighborhood, and professional organizations. The meeting was restricted to those invited; this had the advantage of making sure that most of the public opinion leaders would be there and that there could be no filibuster by any group determined to oppose the plan. The local newspaper was given copies of the maps, charts, diagrams, and other information that had been prepared well in advance of the meeting and was invited to send reporters to cover the discussion.

The initial meeting was followed by three weeks of intensive work by the superintendent, other school officials, and board members. Hardly an evening went by without a public meeting somewhere in the city to discuss the plan. School officials willingly explained the plan and answered questions. The board was not willing, however, to discuss the issue of whether the plan should be adopted or not. It made quite clear from the outset that it had the right to decide, that it was resolved to proceed, and that the public could not stop it from doing so.

Reactions in the white community revealed that on this issue, it was split into two unequal parts. A large segment of the population was in favor of the plan. National and state pressures for action on integration, liberal beliefs among many of the upper middle-class and highly educated citizens, the vocal and active support of the informed segment of the community, and the support of civil rights groups for the plan all combined to produce a large measure of support. The local newspaper also came out in favor of the plan.

A minority in the white community was strongly opposed. A vocal and well-organized group, the Committee on Schools, took over leadership of the opposition. The Committee had been originally set up as a citizens' watchdog over educational expenditures and stood for careful fiscal management. It now made the integration issue one of its vital concerns. The arguments advanced against the plan were those usually voiced against any plan to bus children to achieve racial balance. Regardless of the fact that about two-thirds of public school children of this country are bused to school as a matter of course, opponents argue that busing is unfair to the children involved and harmful to their schooling. In addition, the Committee argued that it would be too expensive and that any additional money could be more effectively spent improving Rochambeau school. Finally, fears were voiced that integration would prove harmful to the white students by lowering academic standards in the receiving schools, while proving ineffective for the black children. The Committee rallied behind it the hard-core opposition of parents who felt threatened by the plan, the racially prejudiced, and all those who were convinced that integration could not possibly work.

The black community was largely silent. The board and

the superintendent constantly conferred with the executive council of the Rochambeau PTA, which had both black and white members, who were invited to help shape the plan being worked out for their children. Neither initiative nor suggestions, let alone opposition, came from the black community at large. In those days, there was little organization among black parents, nor did they feel that any action on their part would produce results. Conversations with parents some years later disclosed that many had been in favor of the plan but that they did not immediately realize that only their children would be bused. White schools, after all, were even more segrated than Rochambeau; it seemed only logical and fair that white children should be bused, too. Feelings became increasingly bitter when it became clear that cross-busing was a political impossibility in White Plains. Indeed, the superintendent attributed part of the success in getting the plan accepted to the fact that it did not necessitate cross-busing. (See Carroll F. Johnson's "Achieving Racial Balance," *School Management Magazine,* January 1968.)

One black mother, asked to comment on the racial balance plan, answered with great contempt. "What racial balance plan? All that we have to date is a plan of convenience—a plan of white convenience. The black community," she went on, "dealing in good faith, opened themselves up to any feasible plan which would bring an integrated school system. . . . but all things are conditional—even securing passage to heaven. The condition here was, as always, that the white community would support a racial balance plan as long as it did not affect their *modus operandi,* their way of life." Such feelings are easy to understand. This particular parent was very much in favor of the idea of integration, but, she said, "Both black and white people should share equally in its implementation." As she sees it, busing black students to white schools only "fosters racism. It supports the theory that whatever is white is right and good. If integration is so damned good," she concluded, "y'all come and get some."

On April 16, 1964, the board met to vote on the plan. The

Committee on Schools, having failed in its call for a referendum on the issue (the board, as it was legally empowered to do, refused to call a referendum), organized a last-minute campaign by letter and telegram urging the board to drop the plan. Supporters rallied around the board and flooded it with mail voicing their approval. When the board voted unanimously in favor of adoption, it received a standing ovation from the supporters in the audience.

Work began immediately to implement the plan. Intensive efforts were made to inform administrators and teachers in the receiving schools about the children who were coming in; a team of educators and psychologists met in regular sessions until the end of the school year in an attempt to anticipate some of the problems that would come up and work out solutions. PTA organizations cooperated by organizing "play days" to acquaint children with their new schools. Finally, as a measure to reassure black parents, a home-school counselor was appointed to explain the plan and to provide a link between the schools and the black community. By September, the school system was ready to operate on the new plan.

I also considered myself ready. I came to teach sixth grade in White Plains in the fall of 1964, after several years' experience in the New York City public schools. I was to work in an elementary school that, until that year, had been entirely white and middle class. Although I knew of the integration plan, I felt no apprehension about it. I had worked with ghetto children before, and I did not think that the situation in White Plains would present any special difficulties. I knew, of course, that the ghetto was vastly different from white suburbia, but, I believed, America is a melting pot after all. I felt quite confident that I would easily be able to deal with any problems that might arise.

THE CHILDREN DEAL
WITH EACH OTHER

It would seem perfectly obvious that if children of widely different backgrounds were put together in one classroom, conflict would result. Nevertheless, this was not at all obvious to me at first. My background was white, middle-class America. Somewhat naively I assumed that my standards and values were acceptable to and even desirable for *all* Americans. I knew that the black children had been deprived of the educational and cultural advantages enjoyed by white middle-class families; I believed that they should be given these opportunities; and I was quite sure that they would profit from adopting the mores and attitudes of my own world.

It was the children themselves who taught me that the problem was much more complicated than that. In my classroom children are always allowed to "be themselves" and to interact freely. Learning to live together, I believe, is a very vital part of education and growth. So I remove myself to the sidelines as much as possible and watch the children handle the situations that come up. As I watched that first year, I learned a great deal.

Bobby was the focal point of much of what went on in class. A thin, pale boy with a thoughtful face, he never spoke unless he had carefully considered what he wanted to say. When he did voice an opinion, it carried weight with everyone. His genuine acceptance of all people and his concern for individuals earned him the liking and respect of all the kids in the class. He had a quiet but keen sense of humor and a strong sense of basic values. He immediately established a very good relationship with me. Many children find the kind of freedom

I offer in the classroom difficult to handle. It was typical of Bobby that he could take on the responsibilities I expected him to shoulder without attempting to infringe on the rights of others.

If Bobby was a natural leader, John was determined to make himself one. Possessed by a driving need to be right, to be first, and to be at the head of the class, he tried frantically to gain a following and to impose his will on all with whom he came into contact. He was the youngest in his family; although he was a very bright boy, he felt overshadowed by a very successful brother and sister and was under a veritable compulsion to prove his own worth. It was almost impossible for him to take any setback or even the mildest criticism from me or from his peers. In class discussions it was John who talked loudest and longest; his shrill voice hammered his opinions home almost brutally in an effort to have them accepted. In his social contacts he was overbearing and domineering with those he considered his inferiors and possessive and jealous of his equals. He was an excellent organizer and could be relied upon to get things done. This and his intellectual ability won him some respect from the class, but no one really liked him with the warmth Bobby was able to arouse.

The girls were led by the "social set." Jane, Joyce, and Brenda formed a group who based its claim to leadership on unassailable middle-class security and an utter inability to recognize and understand any values but their own. They dressed in the latest styles, followed the latest fads, and were caught up in their social plans—future country club matrons all. Jane was entirely uninterested in the academic side of school and was already—at the age of 11—looking about for the right kind of husband. The other two did their school work conscientiously but were more absorbed in their own activities.

Their very imperviousness to any standards but their own made this group a powerful magnet for any girl in the class, particularly for those who were not quite sure of their own social success. Thus, they succeeded in attracting Sue, a shy, quiet girl who had difficulty making friends. Although she was by far their intellectual superior, able and even eager to think and form her own judgments, she began to follow the lead of the group in an effort to become one of them. She was never fully admitted to the inner circle, however, and was only allowed to function as a sort of satellite to the original trio.

Two strong leadership figures emerged from the small black group in the class. Jason, a small but tough, strong, and forceful boy, won recognition from white and black children alike by his powerful personality and aggressive tactics. He did not hesitate to use violence, even against teachers, and was soon feared throughout the school. Deborah, on the other hand, was distinguished by her fearless honesty. Although she felt hopelessly inferior to the white children both in brains and in looks—she usually seemed carelessly dressed, hair un-combed, buttons fastened every which way—she had the courage to speak out on every issue and "tell it like it is," even if the truth was painful.

From the beginning I found this class ready to take a hand in managing its own affairs. One of the problems the children had to contend with was Charlene. No one could overlook Charlene for long or disregard her in any group. A black girl, big for her age, she had a defiant and challenging air about her. Raised in an environment where knowledge of sexual matters comes early, she was self-consciously mature and en-joyed flaunting her sophistication in front of her more shel-tered classmates. She used her superior strength to intimidate all who crossed her path and to get her own way whenever she wanted. In class she was deliberately offensive and dis-ruptive. She would get up and walk around, purposely shock-ing the class and me by loudly abusing us in foul language. She despised and distrusted me, both as a symbol of authority and as a white person. It seemed clear to me that it would be useless to expect her to develop respect for me, either in my professional or personal role. Every attempt to discipline her met with lies, sullen silence, or outrageous insults. Among the white, middle-class children of the neighborhood, she stood out like a sore thumb. To me and to most of the kids she was a constant irritant; no one could remain complacent or self-satisfied with Charlene in the room.

Another problem was Graham; quiet and withdrawn at first, Graham took up a good deal of my attention in class. Like most of the black children in my school, he was very much behind in academic skills, and I had to devote a great deal of energy to helping him. Both Charlene and Graham helped to make us all aware of the difficulties and feelings of the black children in school.

The kids began to discuss civil rights issues. Most of the white students had never fully realized before that these problems existed in their own city. They all knew about discrimination against blacks in the South, but the majority rather vaguely and complacently believed that the North provided equal opportunity for all. Face to face with the realities of an integrated classroom, they began to reevaluate their ideas and to debate the problems of contact between the two worlds.

Their reactions differed widely according to individual personalities. John, for example, experienced a backlash of feelings. He had absorbed from his parents a typically liberal attitude towards blacks. The family had paid lip service to ideas of tolerance and equal rights for all, but not once had they been forced to put these ideas to the test or to make any personal sacrifice to implement them. Now John, with his overwhelming ambition, was made to mark time in class while I worked with Deborah or tried to discipline Charlene. To John, education was the road to success. He became quite frantic at the thought that the black kids might hold him back. Equal opportunity, he believed, had been provided in his city, and it was up to the blacks to take advantage of it;

if they couldn't, they would just have to wait. The idea that *he* might be asked to do something to make it work was completely foreign to him.

"School integration can't work yet," he argued heatedly in one of our class discussions. "The Negro kids aren't ready to work with us, and they can't keep up. First, they will have to bring their education up to ours, then we can work together."

Many of his classmates agreed. Outright bigotry was rare— it was no longer socially acceptable in these middle-class circles to admit to prejudice—but prejudices ran deep. The idea was commonly held that it was up to the black to prove that he was worthy of the opportunities provided for him.

It was here that Sue differed from her friends. While the "social set" was completely insensitive to the problems and feelings of people different from themselves, Sue had an open, loving, and accepting nature, and a family background of genuine commitment to equal rights for all. Unlike John, she did not feel threatened by the black kids, and she was fully aware of the obligations of white people to make a contribution towards a solution of the racial problem.

"I think integration is a good thing," she answered John. "At least we learn to know one another and live with one another. And we do have a lot to learn. I don't want to be like those people in Scarsdale, who let four or five blacks live there and are proud of themselves and think that they have really *done* something!"

Most of the kids became involved in these class discussions, but it was Bobby who was the first one to take action. When I first started to work with Graham, I tried repeatedly to get other boys to help him with his assignments. Most of my efforts came to nothing, because Graham could not relate to other kids. The only one whom he did not completely reject was Bobby, and Bobby decided that my problem with Graham was his problem, too.

What impelled him I don't know. Maybe it was the wordless but nonetheless real relationship that had developed between him and Graham or his basic sense of values that made him feel responsible for another human being. Whatever it was, he came to me one day of his own accord and asked whether I would mind if he tried to help Graham. Such a request had never been made to me before, and it surprised me, even from Bobby. I gladly gave my assent and offered any help I could give.

A very close relationship developed between the two boys. They couldn't have been more different. Bobby came from a secure, if not wealthy, middle-class family; he excelled both in academic work and in sports and was recognized as a leader in the class. Graham came from the projects, was a near-failure academically, and was soon to become notorious for his aggressive and undisciplined behavior. Yet their relationship had none of the patronizing tolerance I had observed in my other classes. Bobby was one of those rare persons who can help without being condescending. Their friendship was "unequal" only in the sense that many human relationships are unequal. Each brought something different to it: Bobby the sincere and honest desire to help, Graham the acceptance needed to make it work. They had genuine respect and liking for each other as human beings and as individuals.

The boys began to work together, and I started to rely on Bobby to keep an eye on Graham and see that he did not get into trouble in school. It speaks volumes for the relationship that Graham did not resent Bobby's assumption of authority over him, as he surely would have resented anyone else's.

It now became possible for Graham to take part in class activities. When the cartoonist for the class newspaper suddenly moved away, Graham's drawing talent made him the logical choice as a replacement. His appointment won general approval, and the newspaper staff, including John, who was editor, all rallied around to show him the ropes and help him meet the deadline.

That winter he had "discovered" skating and had become an addict. This new enthusiasm brought him to the notice of

Linda, the best skater in the class. She was somewhat of a loner herself, and when she heard Graham talk about his progress, she asked him to go skating with her one day. Graham accepted, and the two kids had a very good time together.

Thanks to Bobby, Graham was in some measure becoming a part of the class. Charlene, however, remained a problem. All my efforts to modify her behavior proved fruitless. I moved her from one place to another in an attempt to reduce her nuisance value, but she soon found another way to disturb the class. When I reprimanded her, she would often just walk out of the room. In no instance did she show the slightest inclination to listen or to conform. Among the other kids, she commanded no respect at all. They resented her behavior, which they felt was directed against them, and she had none of the intellectual ability or artistic talent that won recognition for Graham.

Nevertheless, the "social set" decided to do something about Charlene. The girls were particularly outraged by her language, which violated every standard of acceptable behavior in their code. At last they decided that they could no longer tolerate anything as offensive as this. One day after school they waited upon me as a delegation and asked my permission to take Charlene out of the class the next day to talk to her alone. I was doubtful whether they could achieve much but told them to go ahead.

Next day the group took Charlene and left the room. An hour went by and they had still not come back. Just as I was beginning to become apprehensive, they walked in. I never did find out much about that session. When I asked what happened, the girls only said, "At first she laughed, but then she listened." Their unshakeable belief in the validity of their own standards must have come through to Charlene in some way; from that day she modified her language, at least when she was within earshot of her mentors.

Perhaps it was this success, limited though it was, that showed the other kids that something could be done about Charlene. In any case, soon after this, Nancy, one of the meekest girls in the class, suddenly found enough resolution to stand up to her. Nancy was a rather awkward, unpopular girl who had been one of Charlene's main victims all year. Charlene was constantly making loud comments about her in class and had often threatened her physically. This time, however, Charlene went too far; she demanded that Nancy give her her own pen, a treasured possession Nancy did not want to lose. To everyone's surprise, including mine, Nancy swung out and hit her. A fight ensued, which I found myself reluctant to break up; it seemed to me that it was good for Charlene to be shown that she could not get away with everything, just as it was good for Nancy to learn to stand up for herself. Eventually I did intervene to make sure that no one would be hurt. But the incident served its purpose—Nancy soon found that she had gained Charlene's respect as well as the respect of the rest of the class. She also began to think about her experience and to evaluate it. Her conclusions were summed up in this paper, which she submitted to me:

> I think integration in schools is good in some ways, yet bad in others. I myself have experienced integration in my school.
>
> Here are my bad points about integration in the schools.
>
> I think that integration is bad in a way because the Negroes aren't trying to learn in the schools. They all just trying to make trouble in the schools. There are about 500 kids in our school. Out of those 500 kids there are about 100 Negroes in our school. Out of that 100 Negroes there may be 10 Negroes that are making somewhat of an effort.
>
> The Negroes would like to take control. They would like to be leaders. In the time we are in know you have to go to school to learn and try. If they don't try, they will not become good leaders. George Washington Carver tryed and he succeeded. He isn't any different than the negro of today. If he can try others can try. It isn't only the negroes fault for being so bad. The white people reject the negro because he is negro. The

negroe is not a dog he is a person. The negroe isn't any different than the white person. The color shouldn't matter its the person behind it all.

Another reason why I think integration in school is bad is because they scare some white kids at school. The only think of swareing and using their fist to settle things. But do they relly settle the argument? Some negroes think they are big tuff kids. They think that nobody but nobody would dare to hit them. What they need is to be hit back. But there are very few people who would do it. Inside they are cowards.

I have had different incidents when this has happened. Here is one.

At our school there are a fair amount of negroes. I have to admit there are some nice negroes and some bad negroes. These bad negroes pick on kids that they think are weak so they won't hit them back. I have been one of their "victims." Some people think being the negroes' friend will help them avoid them. But being friends won't help at all. If a negroe or a white person starts picking on you. First tell him to stop then If he or she doesn't stop. Shew them to stop. They probably won't bother you any more. Another thing that bothers me is that they have absolutely no respect for anyone. They talk back to their teachers. They talk out in class and they have the nerve to sware at the teachers. They also want to make trouble. They run down the school halls. They act as though they are different then anyone else. They don't have to be told everything individually. What goes for the white people goes for them too.

Here are some good points about integration in schools. I think integration in shcools is good because you get to know the negroe. The negroe is not all bad. If you go to a non-integrated school they have the impression that negroe is all bad, and they call him a Nigger and other things. They really don't know there really like. They really shouldn't say bad things about negroes they really don't know what he is like. But we can voice an opinion on the negroe. We live with him.

whereever you go you will see negroes. Some may be
bad and some may be good.
    People from [non] integrated school should not voice
their opinions. But remember, We Can!

These incidents, different as they were, all confirmed my
original belief that human relations problems in the classroom cannot be solved without the *active* involvement of the
children themselves. Bobby and Graham, Nancy, Charlene,
and the girls all had been learning in their own way to deal
with each other. They could, of course, not all be friends,
but even a clash, such as the one between Nancy and Charlene, is better than the polite tolerance and indifference prac-
ticed when problems are not brought out into the open. If
a teacher settles all problems, order may be preserved, but
nothing real is accomplished. Channels of communication
must be opened and used by the children themselves; the
teacher can only establish the atmosphere in which this is
possible and offer help and guidance when this is needed.

For a while I was much encouraged. If these kids were
really learning to deal with each other as individuals, might
it not eventually become possible to forget about color and
racial attitudes and loyalties and establish a truly integrated
classroom? I was still thinking in terms of the melting pot
ideal. It seemed to me that Charlene was being brought into
the fold and that Graham was finding his place in society.

I soon found that this was a superficial view of the problem;
the children knew better than I.

The class was discussing the nature of prejudice—what
makes people hate like that? This is a difficult question for
11-year-olds to think about. I tried to help. "Have any of
you ever talked to a really prejudiced person about his feelings?" I asked. The answer, surprisingly, came from Bobby.
He looked straight at me from his seat next to Graham's. "I
have," he said. "My father!" He went on to explain that his
father, himself a victim of Hitler's persecution of the Jews,
was prejudiced against blacks. He had repeatedly stated that
he would never hire a black in his business, even if he were

fully qualified. In his quiet way Bobby made it quite clear that he disagreed with his father. It must have cost him a good deal to say this to me in front of the class and in front of Graham. For me, the incident answered a long-standing question in my mind. I had often wondered why the friendship between the two boys was confined to school grounds. Bobby never asked Graham to come home with him. Now I knew.

But it was Graham, it soon appeared, who was grappling with a profounder problem in this relationship. Bobby had to deal with his father's prejudices at home, but he could at least follow his own bent at school. Nothing in his friendship with Graham threatened his integrity or his sense of identity.

Graham, on the other hand, was torn between two worlds and two views of himself to the point where he began to question who he was. He was attracted to Bobby and admired much about him. He valued my good opinion of him and knew that I approved of this friendship; but long before Bobby's confession in class, he knew that this was not where he belonged. He belonged with Jason and his group, with the kids who rode the school bus with him, the tough guys who defied the white world and rejected everything he admired in Bobby. They were demanding that he show where his loyalties lay. Again and again they challenged him to take part in their exploits, and again and again he gave in and joined them.

He was quite unable to cope with this problem, which even an adult would have found difficult to solve. And I was making things even harder for him; I was constantly reproaching him for behaving like Jason and urging him to take Bobby for a model. In effect, I was asking him to become what he was not—white and middle-class. One day, in desperation, he burst out at me, "Who can I be *friends* with then!" I found that I had no answer.

Jason also, for all he seemed so tough and unbeatable, suffered in his own way from the existence of the seemingly unbridgeable gulf between the two worlds. His friendship with Ken was a case in point.

Ken was one of the outstanding boys in the class. A bright student, mature for his age, he had a very strong sense of right and wrong and never hesitated to stand up for what he thought was right. In class, he soon established the kind of relationship with me that Bobby had, but he never allowed this relationship to obscure his judgment. Eyes challenging me from beneath his Beatle haircut, he would come to me to point out where he thought I had been unfair on any issue. Almost always, upon reflection, I found that he was right. He was one of the best students in the class, but had none of John's driving ambition for good grades. Rather, he enjoyed using his intellect, and he had, in addition, a truly engaging wit and sense of humor and a bubbling effervescence that was a joy to watch.

Jason seemed to be the very antithesis of Ken, and that was one of the reasons for the attraction that developed between them. Ken's leadership position was based on his intellect and maturity; Jason was attracted to Ken because he could lead without fighting; Ken had a kind of fearful admiration for Jason's fierceness. They shared a degree of sophistication and a keen sense of humor.

Unlike the relationship between Bobby and Graham, this time Jason took the initiative. When he really wanted something, he went after it with a ruthless and concentrated determination that would not recognize the possibility of defeat. Driven by a need to win at any cost, he would brook no opposition, and this made it almost impossible to withstand him.

What he wanted this time was to be Ken's friend. This meant to him that he had to win Ken over from his secure and remote place in the middle-class world and bring him over to his own side. He began a determined campaign for Ken's attention. Ken, half-flattered, half-afraid, began to respond, but he did not respond strongly enough for Jason. What Jason wanted and needed was to come first in everything with Ken. He refused to work unless he was put in the same group with Ken; if Ken was elected to a committee in the class,

Jason had to be on it, too. If he couldn't get his way peace-
fully, he would try to get it through threats of physical
violence. He became Ken's satellite everywhere, sticking to
him like a leech.

Ken was no match for this kind of concentrated attack. He
was a person who tended to accept other people and he began
by accepting Jason as his friend. Soon, however, the pressure
on him became too great. Like Graham, he felt that he was
being asked to give up his own identity; unlike Graham, he
began to yield. Jason began to demand that Ken adopt the
violent and destructive behavior that he had been exhibiting
in school all along. And Ken could not fight him; slowly his
behavior began to change. He began to join in Jason's clowning in the classroom when he should have been working; both
boys repeatedly got into trouble for uncontrolled behavior in
the gym. Finally, Ken's work began to deteriorate. He was
quite aware of the situation and came into my classroom
several times after school to discuss the problem with me.
He realized as clearly as Graham did that he did not belong
in the "other" world.

The situation came to a head when the next report cards
came out. Ken's mother, concerned by the evidence of his
declining performance, asked the school to transfer her son
to another class, where he would be away from Jason. Ken
agreed to the measure, and for the rest of the year he was in
another group.

Even more than the relationship between Bobby and
Graham, this one was harmful to both boys. Jason, like
Graham, was disappointed in a relationship with a white boy
whom he liked and valued. Ken changed his attitudes towards
the racial issue. Whereas before he had accepted black children genuinely and simply as human beings, he now became
increasingly convinced that they were too different in their
behavior and standards for integration ever to be a real possibility. It was sad to see the change in him.

All these conflicting loyalties and emotions came to a head
at the end of the school year. During the last week of school

we had a field day for the sixth grade. In the boys' race, Bobby was the high favorite, with Jason the runner-up. Excitement ran high when the race started and Bobby took the lead. Suddenly, whether by accident or by design, a scuffle started, and Bobby was hit in the stomach. He was bent over with pain and badly handicapped but finished the race in spite of this. As a result, Jason came in first. The judges had "seen nothing"—it was often easier to see nothing where Jason was concerned—and declared Jason the winner. I felt that this was an injustice to Bobby that I could not let pass. I contested the decision and asked to have the race run again the next day.

Jason, not used to having his will crossed, was furious. The kids, back in the classroom, divided into two camps on the issue, and the lines were drawn according to race. Most of the class knew that Bobby was the better runner; all had seen that he was handicapped; and few could seriously accuse me of racial prejudice (indeed, Jason later admitted to me that he had not believed that I acted from prejudice). Yet, the entire black contingent backed Jason and protested having the race rerun. Graham, too, joined this demonstration of solidarity. On the other hand, all the white children demanded that the race be run again.

Bobby had the hardest time of all. He felt Graham's defection deeply and suffered from the open hostility displayed by the black children. During the demonstration he cried openly. It would probably have been easier for him to have abided by the judges' decision and conceded the prize to Jason. He was frankly afraid of Jason, whose rage was a fearsome thing. But he knew very well that he had not deserved to lose the race. It seemed wrong to back down before a trumped up issue. This was not, in fact, a racial question but one of fairness and justice for all. In the end, Bobby decided to stand up for his rights and joined the demand for a rerun. The next day we held the race over again, and Bobby won by six strides.

Thus the year ended with racial lines in the classroom drawn as firmly as ever. But I think we had all learned something.

The white kids had begun to think about the racial problem and had been forced to recognize its existence. In their dealings with each other, they had had to distinguish between individuals: Graham was clearly different from Charlene, Jason from Deborah. It might be difficult in the future to lump them all together as the "black group." I myself had become aware as never before of the feelings and problems of black kids and of the flaws in prevailing white middle-class values and attitudes. I had been made to realize that there were two Americas in my classroom rather than one and that I must respect the identity of both.

The attraction between Graham and Bobby and Ken and Jason was very real; these friendships foundered on the racial issue. It was to become clear to me in the following year that the racial issue can also be *used* in some cases by children intent on solving personal problems that are basically unrelated to their feelings for the kids whom they befriend.

My new class had none of the cohesiveness and none of the strong leadership of the one the year before. The children subdivided themselves into small cliques, none of which had the unshakeable belief in the validity of their own standards exhibited by the "social set." Neither were there any strong individual leaders. Instead, the group included many children, both white and black, who were extremely unsure of themselves and who had almost no self-discipline nor self-direction.

Byron was a small, very slim, white boy, overactive and slightly frenetic. His overriding need was to be accepted by his peers, but he felt profoundly inadequate to achieve this goal. Because of his size, he could not rely on physical prowess to make his mark, so he tried to do this verbally. In any discussion, on any issue, and even when the class was supposed to be at work, Byron was always talking in an almost compulsive way. Long hair falling into his eyes, his body tense with the need to be heard, unable to sit still and wait his turn, he would voice his opinion on everything under the sun.

Driven by his need to gain approval from the class, he dreaded any identification with the establishment. He made this clear to me very forcefully at the very beginning of the year. We had had a class election, but the elected president did not do her job. I felt compelled to pick a president *pro tem,* and I selected Byron. To my surprise, he refused the position indignantly and sent me the following explanation.

> I am writing this to criticize your policy with the elections. First: it is unfair for you to pick a person. (I'm not saying this because I didn't take the job.) Second: you put people on the spot. At least you put me on the spot. I would love to be Pres. I'd like nothing better. But of all my reputations the one I don't need is that of a teachers pet. By *picking* a president it is like saying then your teachers pet. Already people are starting to think I'm your pet.

Although Byron was very able academically, the kids from whom he sought approval did not consider academic achievement admirable; rather, in this class, it was the "in" thing to *fight* what the school stood for. Thus Byron, although he believed in the value of education, could not bring himself to work as well as he might have. Instead, he turned to the black group of boys in the class, those who seemed to him to be most effective at gaining popularity. They were the ones who were experienced in fighting the school, they were the ones who were experts in showing "sophistication," and they were the ones who were admired for their "manly" powers. To court these boys, Byron began to imitate them. He too would adopt their distinctive loose-limbed "I couldn't care less" walk and their tough talk. Driven by his need to impress the other boys in the class, he thought that his best chance lay in being accepted as one of this group. Unfortunately, he could not succeed in impressing the black boys, who felt that his approach to them was based on reasons that had nothing to do with liking for them as individuals. "I don't like Byron," said Brad to me one day. "He is always trying to be black."

Byron's counterpart among the girls was Karen. Karen too was in desperate need of acceptance. She was living with her father, stepmother, and a new baby; her older sister had left home shortly before she came into my class, and Karen had felt very much alone and rejected at home. In school she tried to gain the respect of the other girls by making herself the "defender of the downtrodden masses." While in private she was willing to concede that I was often within my rights in censuring the black kids, in public she was always on their side, openly accusing me of prejudice every time I tried to reprimand one of them. She, like Byron, imitated their behavior and engaged in disruptive techniques of her own. She would refuse to work, write notes in class, which she ostentatiously passed across the aisle, or slowly amble to the water fountain while I was talking. Capitalizing on the admiration of the class for any flouting of authority, she tried to impress the other children by adopting the ghetto vocabulary; at bottom all this was an attempt to *force* them to admire her.

Her greatest success came when she tried to use the racial issue to rally the other girls around herself in opposition to me. She had begun a genuine friendship with two of the black girls in class, but she began to manifest this in an exaggerated way. The three of them became inseparable, clinging together wherever they went. In the halls Karen would walk arm in arm with both girls, refusing to be separated for anyone. In class she would sit holding hands with one or the other. Whenever I voiced the slightest criticism of either one of the black girls, Karen would make a comment about my prejudice, under her breath but loud enough for the class and me to hear. Soon she succeeded in gaining the support of the other white girls in the class. Even Evelyn, one of the most conservative, middle-class, conforming girls in the group, began to follow her lead and roused herself to make an impassioned speech about how prejudiced I was when I told one of the black girls that she could not walk around freely in class time.

As soon as Karen felt secure enough in her new leadership role for a show of strength, she rallied a group of girls and came to me as the head of a "deputation" to register a formal complaint about my prejudiced treatment of black children.

I saw that Karen would have to be helped to focus on her own problems and face the real issues involved. I told her that I dealt with everyone on an equal basis and that she was not helping the black kids, the class as a whole, or herself by her campaign and her unacceptable behavior.

From then on Karen and I began to hold daily "complaint sessions" at lunchtime, during which I confronted her with her own behavior and with the reasons for it. At first she complained that I was now unfair to her personally; then, although she had previously been totally unable to take criticism, she began to admit that she could be wrong. She started to examine the real reasons for her behavior and slowly she learned to face reality.

If Karen, like Byron, had taken up the cause of the black children to gain acceptance for herself, unlike Byron, she soon developed a real feeling for the girls whom she had befriended. She had a genuine willingness to accept them and a real understanding for them. Unlike Byron also, she was herself accepted by the black girls; indeed, Karen was one of the few neighborhood children who went to the projects after school hours and who kept up a genuine relationship with the black kids in her class.

Experiences such as these convinced me that the racial issue in the classroom cannot be viewed as a problem by itself; it must be handled as part and parcel of the children's whole development and growth. If it was foolish to believe that differences between the two races would disappear in an integrated classroom, it would be just as foolish to forget that every individual will react to any issue according to his own needs. I began to look at my children more closely; what are they looking for and how do they go about getting it? What has shaped them and why do they react as they do?

THE SCHOOL COMMUNITY

Soon after I first came to the school, I began to know many of the children's parents. Those who agreed with my approach to teaching welcomed me warmly, and I soon became a frequent dinner guest in their homes.

The neighborhood population of the school where I teach is middle class and well-to-do to wealthy. Those families who have been secure in the possession of money and status for two generations or more tend to take their wealth and position for granted and are open to liberal ideas for reform and social change. They are vocal and active in community affairs and usually feel relaxed and unthreatened by any rival for their "place in the sun."

Families who are still on their way up in society are generally much more status-conscious and success-minded than their neighbors and are often much more concerned about possible harmful effects on themselves of any program for social change. They tend to distrust innovations.

Living standards in the neighborhood differ slightly, but all families live on the upper middle-class level. Each family has its own home and yard. Each has at least one, often two, cars. The fathers are businessmen, doctors, lawyers, or executives, and in many families both parents have a college education. All plan a college education for their children. Their homes contain bookshelves filled with the latest volumes, and most families subscribe to the most widely circulated magazines and newspapers. Many have taken their children on trips in the United States or abroad, and they all know and use the cultural resources provided by near-by New York City.

Life in these homes is regular and orderly. The whole

family meets at the dinner table, and the children listen to and participate in their parents' conversation. Topics range from their father's business and professional concerns to their mother's PTA and community work, to their own school problems. On many evenings I witnessed spirited discussions on current events and the burning social issues of the day. At the dinner table at Sue's house, for example, I was greatly impressed with a debate on the civil rights issue, in which both children of the family took an active part. Both girls were well-informed on the latest developments and were able to hold their own in the conversation of the adults. Tommy followed events in Vietnam closely and voiced very definite opinions on the subject, based on his readings of *Newsweek* and *Life* magazines as well as on TV news programs. At his house also, the dinner table was the scene of animated conversations on a variety of topics.

A large number of these families have some kind of household help (often black), and many children are used to being served rather than being responsible for some of the chores around the house. A composition of one of my students began: "It was early morning. The laundry had not yet been brought to my room . . ." Many of my pupils tend to look at the adults around them—parents or teachers—as people who exist to help them. They are often demanding and insistent and they become extremely impatient when their demands are not quickly met.

I found many parents in the neighborhood very conscious of their responsibilities as educators. They had given much thought to the problem of how to rear their children and would discuss in great detail their children's problems with me. The parents who agreed with my teaching methods maintained close contact with me and urged me to collaborate with them in solving any problem that might come up. The father of one of my boys even gave me his office phone number so that I could get in touch with him during the working day.

In their relations with their children most of the parents I knew believed that children have a right to an explanation of the rules made for them by the adults around them. For the most part, they did not expect instant obedience to an order but would take the time and exercise the patience to talk over their principles with their children in an effort to win their assent. In some cases parents were so reluctant to "lay down the law" that they could not exert adequate control over their children. Byron's mother, for example, complained to me that she could not get her son to follow *any* direction she gave. Apart from an occasional slap, physical punishment was rare in these families, and children learned at an early age to listen to and follow verbal directions.

All of the parents I knew had great plans for their children and all were keenly aware of the importance of education. They were intensely interested in the school system; many of them had moved to White Plains and to this particular neighborhood because they felt assured of a good education for their children. They were very definite about what they expected the school to provide. They wanted a good academic preparation for college and the best possible teachers, equipment, and books. They were also firmly convinced that their own and their children's destinies lay in their own hands and that they could, for the most part, obtain what they wanted.

Parents from neighborhoods such as this one provide the backbone of community activity on behalf of the schools. They are active in selecting candidates for the school board, organize voters' meetings during the campaign, and man the polling places on election day. They have the time and the inclination to run the PTA. They follow their children's progress and they are quick to appear in school to investigate if things are not going as they should. If they feel that something is wrong, they will not hesitate to blame the teacher or even the principal—both, in their eyes, not representatives of authority but employees paid out of their tax money.

Vivian's parents were typical of this kind of attitude. Vivian had always been an excellent student with an all A report card. She came to my class only for social studies, and she did not do as well as usual with me. On one of her reports

I had to give her a C, because I felt that she had not worked as hard as she could have and that others in the class had done better. Vivian was hurt and upset and told her parents about it that evening. Next day I received a visit from both of her parents, who appeared in school without an appointment. They confronted me angrily, asserting that they could see nothing wrong with the report and demanding that I change the grade. I explained that the paper was fine as far as collecting the information was concerned, but that it did not show any sign of the independent thinking I was sure Vivian was able to do. Only the fact that I taught Vivian only one subject reassured the parents that her record would not be permanently affected.

The children absorb from their parents this serene conviction that the world is their oyster. Tommy, for example, could not understand the white parents in North Carolina who angrily overturned a school bus carrying black children to their school. While we were discussing this incident in class, Tommy voiced his opinion: "My parents wouldn't need to use violence like that," he volunteered. "If my father didn't like a new rule, he would just go to the principal, and if that didn't help, he would go to the superintendent, and if that didn't help, he would go to the school board." Tommy evidently was quite convinced that this would end the matter. The idea that the school board might be able to withstand pressure from his father just did not occur to him.

Children in the white families grow up in an environment where safety and order are taken for granted. As children of well-to-do parents, they have never yet had to face a real struggle. They feel secure and protected by the society in which they live. They are surrounded by things they own— transistor radios, cameras, tape recorders, television sets, bicycles; they learn early to value material possessions. "Get off my property!" shouted the three-year-old brother of one of my students when I came to call.

Many of these children are extremely status-minded and money-conscious. Success for them is of great importance, and their sense of competition is keen; but success is recognizable only when it is expressed in tangible, material terms. Their ambitions are to become businessmen or professionals like their fathers, and most of them are planning to make a lot of money when they grow up. Their lives untouched by the problems of the world around them, they are confident in the belief that their only duty is to themselves. Nothing, they feel, should be allowed to stand in the way of their success.

In their views on the integration issue, these neighborhood families differed widely, ranging from dedicated work to get the plan adopted in the community, to hard-core opposition. Some of the leaders in the Committee on Schools live in this area. The opposition, however, was a minority in the neighborhood, and the plan was publicly welcomed by most of the families. Among its supporters, however, there were only a few who fully understood the problems involved. It was widely believed at the time—just as I believed initially—that we needed only to open the doors of the white schools to black children and "let" the ghetto students adapt. It is symptomatic of this attitude that, when preparations were being made for implementing the plan, a home-school counsellor—a black man —was appointed only for the black community. It occurred to no one that it might be necessary to explain black attitudes, feelings, and mores to the whites. Out of touch with the mood of the black population, few of the white families realized that it might be impossible or undesirable for black children to adapt and that they might not even want to. Most were still imbued with the "melting pot" concept of America, which holds that our society had blended and welded its disparate elements together, that we are producing one homogeneous whole, and that all necessary adjustments could be made easily. Only after integration and with the events that took place in American society during the sixties, did the white community come to realize the existence of the deep cleavage between white and black communities.

Equally unexpected to most families was the reaction of many middle-class children to the new situation in the schools.

Far from becoming reinforced in the liberal beliefs in which most of them had been raised—that all men are born equal and that prejudice is bad—children began coming home with complaints about the behavior of the ghetto kids. Some, like Nancy, were beaten up; others, like John, were worried that they were being held back while the class had to wait for the ghetto students to catch up. Some became contemptuous of their black classmates; others began to imitate the vocabulary and manners of the black children. Papers written in my class clearly showed the resulting conflict:

> My progress with the Negroes has been poor. Most of the time it has been the Negroes falt but I also start in sometimes. For example: one day in math I said to Brad I know your spelling mark and he said shut-up you "Red-Headed Monkey" and if you were in my place it would be hard to control yourself. Sometimes they go to far. My freind had a project in science his razor was stolen and my freind caught a negroe with it. The negroes always have to have more than me, and always more than whites. In the negroes life they have use force to fight their way throught life. I dont understand why they dont use peaceful means, I have great difficulties with many of the negroes some are: When they need money and I say I do not have any they have to check me and always get made if I don't have any. For example: I had a bunch of pennies and Luke wanted them I said no and he said Ill flip you coins I did and won he wanted them back we repeated it again I won and he wanted it I said "I gave you a chance" so I am sorry he was mad I went to the bathroom and he followed and started a fight I stood there till I was fed up and threw him against the wall he was crying, he got a gang on me and started mugging me. To sum all this up, I do not think that I have done very well with getting along with Negroes and whites will both agree that all other men are created equal and none shall let the other fall, witch means that you should help the other if he is in trouble.

Another child commented:

> Most of the white boys and girls in grade 3-6 are
> mature enough to realise that skin color does not make
> a difference in your brain. I have hear some children
> though in the younger grades saying: "Ugh, hes black
> so he must be dumb. This is a minor problem, and
> most likely their opinions will change when they grow
> up. . . . . . Another problem, not so big, is bullies on
> the playground I think part of this is because they
> realise they can't beat the white kids academically so
> they try to beat them physically. The other part is
> their envirment, bigger kids are always bullying them,
> so when they see a boy smaller than themselves, they
> bully him . . . Our school still has a long way to go to
> have their integration system perfected, but I think one
> day they can do it, and if America folowsin its foot-
> steps it will make our country a better place to live in!

These reactions dismayed parents who did not want their
children to develop prejudice but who were also shocked by
the behavior exhibited by the black kids. The parents themselves began to experience very real and painful confusion
and conflict between ideas and principles in which they genuinely and deeply believed and the unpalatable facts of the
realities in school.

Conflict was aggravated when well-intentioned, but often
misguided, attempts were made by neighborhood families to
become acquainted with black parents and draw them into
the life of the school. These efforts came up against the
economic facts of life. Black parents lived at the other end
of town, and transportation was not available. Most black
families did not own a car, and coming to meetings in school
involved the expense of a taxi both ways. Since most mothers
in the projects have to work, it was impossible for them to be
active on PTA boards, which meet in the middle of the working day. Offers by white PTA members to provide car pools
for evening meetings were unwelcome, since they smacked

too much of patronage. Few in the black community wanted to be indebted to a white person, however well-meaning the offer. White parents meeting these rebuffs and failures began to feel frustrated and disillusioned, and misunderstandings abounded.

One black mother related indignantly to me her experience with the PTA at my school. She had held a position on the board and had attended meetings regularly. The expense of the taxi was shared with a friend and neighbor, who also sat on the board. Both women felt—rightly or wrongly—that their presence on the board was "token" and that the white members did not want to listen to their opinions or suggestions. In the middle of the school year, one of the women found that she would have to go to work and had to resign her position on the board. This left her friend to bear the cost of the taxi alone. A few days later, the PTA president called the remaining black member. "We have found a job for you to do that will not involve your attendance at school," she announced. She may have been under the impression that she was rendering a service by solving the transportation problem. What the black mother heard her say was "We have solved the problem of having a black mother on the board— we will have her perform a meaningless job out of sight of anyone else." She lost no time in resigning from the position.

It was difficult for white families to admit to these problems and to face them honestly. Open discussion of the difficulties involved sounded too much like racial prejudice. Some experienced a backlash of feeling, born of disappointment. They began to assert that the black kids were just "impossible," that they were rejecting the advantages offered them, and thus they succeeded in rationalizing a desire to forget about the whole issue. Others staunchly insisted that there was no problem with the integration program, that everything was going smoothly, that the children were becoming friends with one another, and that the plan had achieved exactly what it had set out to do. This too left nothing more to be said. Only a few came to the same realization I had come to: the issues must be faced and openly dealt with if anything constructive was to be achieved.

For me it had been easier to reach this conclusion, since I had to face the problem every day in class. But I too was insensitive to the feelings of the black community until I was forced by my students to make an effort to see things from the ghetto point of view.

My first personal experience of the gulf between the two worlds and the depth of the distrust between them came when I visited Graham's home for a talk with his mother. Graham was becoming a problem for me in class, and, since his mother worked all day and could not come to school, I resolved to ask to see her at home one evening.

There is no denying the fact that I was somewhat apprehensive about my reception in the ghetto. I had never been inside the projects before and, when I arrived there, I discovered that I was nervous. My unease mounted when I found the entrance surrounded by a group of teen-age boys, all unknown to me. For the first time, I had an inkling what it must feel like to the black children in school to enter a predominantly white world every morning. There was no reason for me to think that the boys were unfriendly; nevertheless, I felt conspicuous and I was sure that they were wondering what I was doing there. Quite groundlessly I became afraid that they would not let me pass or would challenge me in some way and I had no idea how I would act if they did. My inner tension eased when a group of younger children who knew me from school ran up to say hello. The older boys moved aside to let me pass.

The interior of the building came as a shock. The halls were dirty, and the elevator was littered with broken toys. A pervasive unpleasant smell was everywhere.

But some of my apprehension vanished when I rang Graham's doorbell, and his mother opened the door for me. A small, heavy-set woman, she welcomed me warmly and led the way into the apartment. The rooms were small and cramped but very neat. Mrs. S. was eager to make me feel at home. Far from showing any constraint, she talked volubly, making it quite clear that she took an interest in Graham's progress in school and that she was glad I had come.

I too was glad that I had come. I was learning much that explained Graham's personality and his problems. He was, I found, one of a family of 13 children. His father—whom I never met—was a strict disciplinarian, an extremely religious man with rigid ideas about obedience. Graham's mother was a houseworker and could not be at home with the children as much as she would have liked. She did her very best for them, however. There was always a meal left for them on the stove if she could not be at home in time for dinner; it was she who provided transportation for Graham to go to his art classes, even though this often represented a considerable financial sacrifice. She had a warm personality and was the source of all the love and human contact for Graham at home.

Three of the children still lived at home—Bill, a teen-ager, a sister in junior high school, and Graham himself. One of the older sisters lived in town and worked in one of the social agencies. She showed an intermittent interest in Graham; nevertheless, by force of circumstances, he was not receiving enough adult attention and was left far too much to his own devices.

This visit gave me my first insight into the problems of ghetto families. I have since tried to establish contact with a number of the families of my black students and, most of the time, I have been well received. It was for the most part, difficult, however, to build up the comfortable relationships I succeeded in forming with many of the white parents.

The black population of the school is all drawn from the projects or from the surrounding area. All families live in cramped apartments like Graham's and must often crowd together in space much too small for them. The projects are high-rise buildings, so that about 200 children are concentrated in an area of about two city blocks. The playgrounds are small, and recreation facilities in the ghetto area are inadequate. There are a few small basketball courts, but no swimming pool, no ball field, and no tennis courts, so that children are forced to fight for their chance at the swings, the basket, or the other equipment.

Like Mrs. S., most of the mothers of my black students work, and children remain unsupervised or are supervised by other children not much older than themselves. Deborah was responsible for her younger brothers during the time she was not in school and spent most of her vacations babysitting for them. With space at a premium in the apartments and with members of the family coming home at different hours, family life is much different in the projects from that in the school neighborhood homes. A leisurely, quiet meal and conversation over the dinner table are impossible. Many of the families I knew were fatherless, and mothers coming home tired from a day's work were faced with turmoil: small children had to be attended to, the laundry was waiting to be done, or the baby was crying. In addition, the walls of the apartments are thin, and the neighbor's TV or a fight between the boys next door are as loud as if they were in the same room.

Child-rearing methods in these families are determined by the harsh living conditions as much as by the ghetto culture. Children are early held responsible for the chores of the household; Deborah had to wash dishes and mind the younger children, Kency had to take out the garbage, Ted was sent to do the shopping for his mother. Parents expect instant obedience to their commands—no one has the time or patience or inclination to explain or persuade. If a child does not obey, punishment is swift and takes physical form. "Do you want me to use the belt?" was a threat Deborah's father used to keep her little brother quiet. I never saw the belt used, but neither parent hesitated about slapping a recalcitrant child.

Most black parents have little education, and few hold the kind of job that inspire their children to make an effort in school and with ambition to succeed. Poor families do not buy many books or subscribe to magazines and newspapers, and the children for the most part lack the kind of intellectual stimulation the white children receive at home.

The world at large looks quite different to black children than to the white. Life outside the apartments is neither safe nor orderly. Violence and physical force is very much a part of these children's lives from a very young age. Deborah told me that her mother would not let her go outside to the playground by herself until she was sure that she could defend herself. Now Deborah was teaching her three-year-old brother to fight and was seriously worried because he didn't take to it. Kency is a prey to nameless fears. He likes the new candy store on the corner of his street. "It's neat, it's my favorite store," he told me. "Oh, I *hope* they don't burn it down!" (This was during the summer of the Newark riots in 1967, which he watched on television until his mother made him turn off the set.) All kinds of scary things may happen at any time, he knows: "I can hear them throwing around the lids of the garbage cans at night," he said, "but I just go under the blankets."

In this world of violence and fear, there is no help but self-help. White children are taught that the policeman is their friend and that society exists to protect them. The black kids learn that all established authority can be the enemy; it may be placated, fooled, or defied—but never trusted.

The school, to the black community, is part of the white establishment. Black parents feel that their children must be steeled for battle before they send them to class. "They must be strong," said one mother to me, "so that they can stand up to the pressure the school will put on them. Teachers will make them feel inferior, and white children will put them down. They must know who they are and that they are somebody, so that they won't believe all the things the white world will tell them about themselves."

Black parents are just as concerned about their children's education as the neighborhood white families. They too want the very best the system can provide. With more job opportunities beginning to open up for blacks, there is a growing realization that education is important and that it can lead to a better life. They would like to see more of their children go to college; they would also like to see better vocational training programs provided for those who will not. Unlike the white parents, however, black parents have not felt that they are in a position to exert any influence on school policy. It is not their taxes that pay for the schools, and it is not their candidates who sit on the school board. Indeed, some in the black community are convinced that any candidate nominated by blacks will *ipso facto* be defeated. When it comes to shaping policy, they are not the doers of society; they are the ones to whom things are done. They mostly simply assume that they would not be heard. "It takes one white parent's phone call to get the principal to censure a teacher," one black man said to me, "but it would take about seventy of us to go up there in a body, to get the same thing done for one of us." (They go "up" to the school board and "down" to the projects.) Right or wrong—and often they may be wrong—this is the view from the projects.

To many of these parents, the principal, the superintendent, and even the classroom teacher are still authority figures, and they will hesitate to openly criticize them. If something goes wrong in school, the tendency is to blame the child rather than the teacher.

These attitudes are just beginning to change. Black parents have learned to organize and to voice their demands. In a recent confrontation with the school board, they succeeded in modifying a revision of the busing plan in their favor. Some do now complain to the principal. But feelings of mistrust are too deeply rooted, and black people have been deceived too often by white promises for them to have much faith in anything American society sees fit to offer them. "How can this be used to keep us down?" is the question automatically asked about every new measure. These attitudes, vocal or silent, are transmitted to the children before they come to school. They are very much on guard when they venture out into the white world.

BEHAVIOR PATTERNS AND
SURVIVAL TECHNIQUES:
Children Deal with the School

With my increasing awareness of the gulf that exists between the two worlds, it began to appear completely unrealistic to me to expect both groups of children to react to the demands of the school in the same way.

School, I found, means widely different things to the children of the two races. For white children, it is a part of their own neighborhood. They come every morning from their homes, walking, riding their bicycles, or in cars driven by their mother or by a neighbor. They come, most of them, slowly, relaxed, at their own pace. The distance they cover is short, both realistically and psychologically. They cross no boundaries and make no journeys. The school is an extension of their homes. It is, they feel, an institution put there for them, where they can learn what will be useful to them in their future lives.

What is school *for* in their eyes? Ask them that question, and they will answer promptly and readily: "School gives you an education." Probe a little more deeply, and you will elicit responses that will differ according to individual attitudes. "An education," says Tommy, a thin, dark, intense boy with an immense desire to succeed, "is needed to get into a good college." Why does he want to go to a good college? He thinks that is a pretty silly question. "To have a better career, of course." "Yes," I persist, but what is a "better career?" That's easy. "It's when you make more money."

Tommy's opinion is shared by many others. Children writing on the subject had this to say:

I come to school because my mother makes me usualy she is nice to me, she also wants me to learn and have a good education and when I grow up be able to get a good job. The only reason I come to school is to learn so when I grow up I can get a good and not bad job.

The reason I come to school is because when I grow up I want to be an architect.

I come to school because I would like to get a good education. I also come so that some day when I am older I will be able to get a good job. Another reason why I come to school is because my parents make me. I am glad that they do because some day they would like to see me get a good job and also see me go to a great college.

I come to school because my father makes me and I know I have to. He said, you go to school to get a good education so you can get a job and earn money to support yourself.

This is my honest opinion. I come to school for an education for ability for later years. To get a job, to earn money by my job for my family I hope to have.

For some, like Sue for example, the word "education" has a different meaning. She comes from a family deeply involved in intellectual interests and in the problems of today's world. She wants to "understand more." "Understand what?" I asked. "Why there is a war, and pollution and things like that," she said. Quite simply, she wants to understand the "why" of everything.

Even the dissidents, the children who find school a bore and a "drag," do not feel that it is entirely unnecessary.

I come to school to learn. I know I enjoy not coming to school because of sickness, holidays and weekends. But I realize that to get a good job and have a happy

productive life you need an education. Some days in
school have been unhappy, dreary and bord. This
really adds up to face life.

Not all are so philosophical about it:

I think that school should be two and a half hours
long and since we can't I think that playground should
be longer. And we need more to eat. I think we don't
need english, that much, and not to much spelling.
Music should be more modern—I think its okay besides
all that.

Even the severest critics, however, find some sense in going
to school:

I go to school because my mother makes me. I do not
like my school. I would like school with less children
for there is to much noise here. I could also learn
better. I want to have a good education but in a
fun way.

Young as they are, all these white children have goals in
mind for their own future and most of them feel fairly secure
in planning to achieve them. Right or wrong, they agree on
the basic point: school is good for something. Even if they
are bored with it or scared of it, they accept the idea that it
offers them something they will need in their later lives.

In reality, of course, it does much more than that. It is the
place where they spend a very large part of their days, the
center of their social life, and the focus of their growth. It
is here that friendships are formed, it is here that they can
impress their peers, and it is here that they can try out their
skills in living. School meshes with their home environment;
they see here the same children they see on their street, they
play with each other after school hours, and they go to the
same church or temple. School is an integral part of their
whole life.

This is not to say, of course, that *all* white children can
deal with the school as it is nor that none has his or her

doubts and problems with it. Richard, for example, dreaded coming to school every morning. He saw it as an immense threat to his personality, because he was *sure* that he couldn't possibly ever succeed in doing anything demanded of him there. Every instruction from the teacher made him feel that he would be exposed in front of his peers as utterly incompetent and that he would be destroyed as an individual. As a result, he fought the rules and regulations at every step of the way. He "forgot" his assignments, he "lost" his paper, he "couldn't find" the right page in the book. He had an impressive vocabulary for his age and great skill in using it. In an effort to make me appear ridiculous in front of the class, he would overwhelm me with a flood of sarcastic and well-reasoned arguments or would note pointedly every time I forgot to put a comma where it belonged in the sentence on the board. In short, he fought the school in every way he knew how, and the fight was a fight for his own survival.

Steve came from a broken home and lived with his mother. He suffered from a great sense of insecurity, and this showed up in school in the way in which he was constantly testing the limits I had set. Any rule I made and any instruction I issued was met by Steve with a flat refusal to comply. It took constant effort to make him follow through and to make him realize that if he did not, he would have to take the consequences of his actions. If I asked for a homework assignment, Steve would not bring it in; if I then gave him a failing grade for the work, he would start an indignant argument. If I asked him to be quiet in class in order to give other students a chance to voice their opinions, he would continue to talk so that I would have to take him to task over and over again. All the time, Steve was asking me to set limits for him, which I would not let him ignore. He needed someone to show enough interest in and concern for him to take the trouble to enforce the rules. At the same time he was fighting the school, he was really asking for some security for himself—he *wanted* to be shown that there were really some things he could not do.

Bill was another boy who found it difficult to adapt to school. He was a poor student, lagging far behind his grade level in basic skills. He found it impossible, however, to admit this, even to himself. Every time I assigned some work for other children, Bill would demand to be allowed to do it too: "I know how to do it," he would insist, although he found out again and again that his attempt would not succeed.

His most serious problem in school was that he could not relate to other children. Like Steve, he seemed to lack self-control and was accustomed to having his own way at home. It was impossible for him to wait for his turn or to defer, even for a few minutes, the gratification of any wish that might occur to him. He became extremely aggressive when he was balked in his desires, using his chunky strength to push the other children out of the way and hitting out angrily at anyone who would not let him do what he wanted. If he wanted to play a game, he had to play immediately. He would not hesitate to interrupt other children in the middle of something they had started just because he could not bring himself to wait. If he wanted to talk to me or needed the answer to a question, he would interrupt anything that might be going on in class. As a result, other children did not want to have anything to do with him, and he was almost completely ostracized in class. To compensate, he would project an aura of "supersophistication," making off-color remarks under his breath, but loudly enough for the kids and me to hear, or daring me to object to a record of *Hair* he brought to school.

For one reason or another, these white children all saw themselves in a very poor light and suffered from it; none of them could deal successfully with the school and all of them felt compelled to fight it. The reasons for their behavior, however, were to be found in their own personalities, in their individual backgrounds, and within their private lives. These were problems I expected and to which I had become accustomed. I dealt with them as best I could. Although it was, of course, not always possible to be successful, I could at least meet these children on a ground common to both of us. They were still within the mainstream of the school; they accepted me and my standards, even if they did not conform to them. Their battles were their private concern; they were not *doomed* to fight.

For black children, however, the situation is entirely different. It is my suspicion that if you asked black children what school is really for—what they really *feel* school is for—they would be stumped for an answer. "You've got to go to school to get an education," they said glibly, when I asked them. But what *is* an education and what is it for? Here they do not seem to be too sure.

Brad could be a good student, but he refused to work. Annoyed with this attitude, I urged him repeatedly to work harder. "What's the use?" he asked. "I'm not a good enough athlete to go to college." He was convinced that black students do not go to college for their intellectual merits. Kency, a thin, slight, physically weak boy, wants to be a football player when he grows up—this is his idea of success within his reach. Laurel wants to be a teacher. "Yes, but you have to go to high school for that," Kency reminded her, seeing this as a hurdle. He knows too many who drop out.

School children are brought up on the American dream: work hard and you will succeed; be ambitious and you will be rewarded; there is equal opportunity for everyone; success is attainable for all; and the race goes to the swift. This may no longer apply to our society today, but many still believe it. I, too, was embued with these attitudes, and the white children in my school saw no reason to doubt them. Why should they? After all, they are the children of the "swift," they belong to those who are winning the race, and they are getting ready to take over the world from their parents.

For the first time I tried to see America as it is seen from the ghetto. Black children, I found, do not listen to the dream. They know—from bitter personal experience and from the lives of their parents and grandparents—in their very bones that there is no such thing as the American dream for them, and never has been. Their parents, far from winning the race, were not even allowed to enter it. Almost none of the things we teach in our schools about America—from the recital of the Pledge of Allegiance in the morning to the blowing of taps for the lowering of the flag in the afternoon—have relevance to them.

How can they look on education as the ladder to success, when they see white faces filling almost every important position? How can they work hard and believe in the future, living as they do in the ghetto which teaches that one cannot plan for tomorrow? How can they believe that effort will be rewarded, surrounded as they are by poverty?

They come to school because their parents want them to go, because it is the law, because it is the thing for children to do. But this school, for them, is an alien place.

They come in a big, yellow bus, and although the trip may last only a few minutes, it is a long journey. They *do* cross boundaries on their way. From the beginning of the school day to the end, they are set apart. They cannot set their own pace for coming to school—they must rush for the bus. They arrive in a group, often a few minutes after the other children have settled down in the classroom. They leave later than the rest, and they have to wait for their bus, supervised by an impatient teacher anxious to go home. They are distinct from the others—the "bus children."

Once in school, they are in a strange world, hostile, dangerous, and unpredictable. "I don't like this school," complained a third-grader, trying to voice his discomfort. "It has no stairs!" Darlene listened to a monster story. "Fear," she said "that's just like me." Scared and exposed, she looks for security. In class she always sticks closely to Verna, in search of comfort and warmth. Every time the class organizes a group activity, the two girls quietly get up and go and sit together in a remote corner of the room—they feel safer that way. One of the black girls voices in an essay her nostalgia for a school where she could feel at home:

A School

> This is a school [little drawings accompany the text] a school that was once a nice school. You would be surprise in how this school was made its walls were nice and strong and the roof in some places it would leak. But it was alright anyway. Most of the time we would just keep on walking by the leak. The rooms were nice and strong and if you kick the walls you would hurt your feet. There was a piano in some of the rooms some of them would fall apart if you play them. In some parts of the school it was weak and in some parts it was strong. But it was a good school.

The sense of this is unmistakeable—the roof may leak, the pianos might fall apart, but she could feel at home in such a school, not like the one she is in now.

For black children, school is not an extension of their home environment. There is a very sharp break between their private lives and their school day. They ride the buses with their friends and neighbors, but in their classes there are just a few children from their neighborhood. During the school day they must try to adjust to a world and a culture in which they have no real part; most of their social life, their growth, their development, their *living* takes place in their own world, outside the school. There are a few cases of friendships between black and white children that carry over into after-school hours. I witnessed some very good relationships. Jimmie and Ben, for example, began working together as a team in class. Ben, a white boy, was helping Jimmie, who is black, and both were learning from the experience. From the classroom relationship they developed a very real friendship. Ben invited Jimmie to his home, where he was welcomed and made to feel at ease. Marva and Ann were another such example;

Marva received help from Ann in school, and the friendship endured after school.

Such cases, however, are unfortunately rare. With Jason and Ken and Graham and Bobby, I saw how difficult it was for real relationships to develop and last between children of such widely different backgrounds and experience. I came to realize that most black children must suffer through that part of the day they spend in school.

As a group, they *were* doomed to struggle. They had to deal with a system that was trying to make them over in its own image and refused to recognize their separate identity. I was making demands that they conform and be *like* everyone else, while at the same time constantly reminding them that they were *unlike* everyone else. The personal problems they had to solve were rooted in the nature of American society as much as in their individual backgrounds. They had to fight, if only to stay spiritually alive. I began to see the behavior of black children in school as part of their fight for survival rather than as nonconformity and senseless defiance.

Their battles took on different forms, according to their individual personalities. Many of them chose head-on confrontation or violence. Charlene gloried in her open defiance of white middle-class standards of behavior and morality. Jason sought recognition through the use of physical force. He would hold up other children in the halls and in the cafeteria, asking them to hand over their money and threatening to administer a beating if they refused. In the school yard he was king. One winter he established himself on top of a snowpile and exacted fees from everyone who wanted to play with the snow. Black and white children, all were afraid of him; he did not even hesitate to attack teachers. Brad tried to control the world by playing games according to his own rules. "When he doesn't like the way things are going for him, he just changes the rules," complained the other children. It is as if he were saying, "It is me who is running things around here for a change!"

Some preferred means less open and far more difficult to deal with. They might withdraw from their surroundings and just sit out the school day until it was time to go home. Luke, for example, would sit in his seat, his face drawn into an angry frown, unresponsive to any attempt to involve him in what is going on. Dorothy saw possible salvation in trying to be as much like the white middle-class ideal as possible. She came to school immaculately dressed, every hair in place, books in plastic covers, pencils sharpened; but she would walk down the halls stiff as a wooden figure, her elbows pressed to her sides, holding herself as erect as she can. She never raised her voice above a whisper, rigid with the effort to melt into the background. The tension surrounding her was almost palpable. Dorothy's reaction was one way of "keeping up with the Joneses."

Many of the black kids felt acutely the great difference between the white children's standard of living and their own; this is only natural, especially in our society, which values material possessions as symbols of status and success. To bridge the gap, some children would make up elaborate stories about trips they took and presents they received, just to impress their white classmates and make themselves feel good. Ted gave me a circumstantial account of his trip to Florida during Easter vacation, including a detailed description of the luxurious motel suite he occupied—alone. When challenged he admitted with his ready smile that this was taken from a TV program he had watched. Far from impressing the white children, such stories usually succeed in annoying them. "If I say I am going to Florida or somewhere else, they have to be big and go on a better vacation," said Peter in disgust, when he was trying to analyze his own attitudes towards his black classmates. Very few black children are ready and willing to talk openly and honestly in class about their homes and their families—a sad comment to make about ten-year-olds!

Another category of survival techniques is the tactic of using the racial issue to defend oneself and to win in the fight against the school. Many of the black children will accuse the teacher of racial prejudice—whether they really believe it or not—in order to manipulate a situation in their favor. Jason, for example, accused me of being prejudiced when I insisted that the race with Bobby be run over again. Charlene and her mother were sure that my efforts to curb her disruptive behavior stemmed from prejudice.

It is in this type of situation that a white teacher is at a distinct disadvantage. It is difficult for black parents and children alike to trust a white teacher and to believe that he is not trying to be vindictive when the children are reprimanded.

One of the more constructive aspects of the black children's struggle for recognition of their separate existence is the current popularity of Afro haircuts and the new awareness that "black is beautiful." Although this awareness cannot be expected to succeed overnight or wipe out centuries of self-depreciation on the part of the black population, these attempts to assert the positive value of being different are healthy and should be encouraged. It was, I knew, a sign of growth and increasing strength, when Deborah began writing poems like the one on page 57.

Afro haircuts, African styles of dress, and an increasing militant stance on racial questions all may violate white middle-class standards of behavior; in my black students I knew I had to welcome them as a sign of increasing self-respect.

What I came to realize was that much of the behavior of the black children in a predominantly white school is part of an attempt to keep themselves *intact*. For these children, as a group, these techniques represent a vital need, and they feel that they cannot operate without these protective devices.

The problem is how to deal with them. Many of these behavior patterns are extremely irritating to the teacher as well as to the other children. Often they are destructive to both

I'm Black and I'm Me

I'm Black and I'm me
I know you wish you were just like me
I wear an afro and wear it proud
As the white man looks and gathers a crowd

You're jealous because I am to be
But I'm Black and I'm me
Can't you see White man, White man
I just laugh when you get a sun tan

But when your black like me
You look up proud as to say "look at me"
My beautiful skin from ancestors
And look at and your sun blisters

the black children and to the school as a whole. Violence, fighting, disruptive behavior, and an unwillingness to abide by the rules are unacceptable in any organized community. Recognition of the reasons for this kind of behavior does not mean that it can be tolerated.

The trouble in a school such as mine is that the black children are not in the mainstream of school life. While white problem children may be difficult for a teacher to handle, rarely are they viewed as outcasts. Black children, reacting to the pressures that they conform to the standards of the majority, are waging an unorthodox battle. It is all too easy for a teacher, himself a member of this majority, to reject this black group as a whole as "impossible" and to avoid dealing with them altogether. The first reaction often is to just remove disruptive students from the class and let them be dealt with elsewhere. Look into the main office of the school at almost any hour of the day, and you will see at least one or two black faces—children sitting out a period of banishment or waiting for an interview with the principal before they are allowed to go back to the classroom. The only alternative to this, it seems, is a head-on collision between the teacher and the black students; it is hard to see how else they can be made to conform.

It took me months of hard learning before I was able to see Charlene's obscenities, Jason's violence, and Brad's defiance for what they really were. It was at this point that I came to realize that it was vitally important, particularly when dealing with a black child, to handle as many problems as possible in the classroom. The class is a living whole; any crisis or problem that comes up affects all of us in the group. If black children are to become an integral part of the class, the behavior they present to the teacher should be handled in the presence of all concerned. Moreover, if part of the black child's struggle against the school is a struggle to survive, exile from the classroom must help to confirm his view that he is indeed invisible to the white world. If the teacher does not react to the challenge the child is offering, the student must feel that he does not really exist. He is asking to be seen and to be heard—he must not be ignored. I came to the conclusion that confrontation is necessary, just as long as it is not punitive. Like all other children in the classroom, black kids must be taught—firmly, patiently, and consistently—how far they can go and where the limits are.

THE SCHOOL DEALS
WITH THE CHILDREN

The question is: how far *can* children go? How much conformity can or must teachers insist on, and how do we do this without destroying individuality or group identity?

Individual children work out their own ways of dealing with the school. School authorities mostly have very definite and standardized ideas on how to deal with children. Discipline is one of the main concerns of every school; much of the time of teachers and administrators is spent on problems of control. Throughout all my years as a student and as a student teacher, this is the idea I was taught to accept—discipline means control. It exists for the convenience of the adults in the school. It consists of a set of rules imposed on the children by the grown-ups; the children are expected to accept them and obey without question. The consensus is that only in this way can the school hope to preserve law and order.

At the same time we were told that one of the main functions of the school is to mold the citizen of the future. It is here we teach the children to adapt to the society in which they live. And what do we teach the citizens of the future? Obedience is an important virtue; it is wrong to question higher authority; children who do not conform and obey are punished; and those who succeed best in accepting the system are put into positions of control in their turn—they are charged with keeping their classmates in line. Hardly ever have I heard the question raised: does not a society such as ours *need* the nonconformist, the responsible critic, the independent thinker?

Once I began teaching on my own, I began to ask myself

what discipline is *really* for and whom it should serve. It seemed to me that a teacher who cannot get children to work without the threat of punishment must be doing something wrong. Control imposed from above breeds apathy and sullenness at best; at worst, it generates resentment, rebellion, and discontent. Law and order that are maintained by the threat of force is no order at all; it will collapse as soon as the child feels stronger than the person or institution set to control him.

My ideas on discipline are closely related to my ideas on teaching. In my experience a quiet classroom, full of children sitting still in their seats, respectfully "listening" to the teacher is usually a dead classroom—no learning of any significance will take place. The children may not seem to be doing anything else while the teacher is talking, but chances are high that many of them are not listening at all; the only thing they will be learning is how to conform and how to get along with the adult world.

Discipline to me is meaningless unless it comes from within. It is something that must be learned, and this is part of the process of education and growth. It must benefit the child rather than the teacher; good citizens in our society are not the conformists who never question but merely obey; rather, they must be people who know how to weigh discussions and make their own judgments.

The essential factor in school is that the teacher must set only the general framework; children must be trusted and encouraged to form their own opinions, find their own solutions, and regulate their own behavior.

If discipline is something that must be learned, it should also be taught, and the way to teach it is to let the children practice it. The longer I teach, the more convinced I become that it is essential to let children learn from their own mistakes. But it takes courage and faith in kids to let them make mistakes.

Every year teachers in my school meet to select the children who will be monitors next fall. There is usually general agreement that the job should go to those children who have been commended for good and responsible behavior. I found myself alone in the view that—as one colleague put it—"the appointment should go to those who need it for therapy." I do indeed believe that the monitor jobs should be reserved for those who need training in responsibility and decision-making, not for those who already have these skills.

The mother of one of my students told me in some dismay one day that she had come to school to visit and had been unable at first to even see her son. To the uninitiated observer, my classroom looked like sheer chaos; everyone was doing something different. Children were coming and going, some were sitting on the floor, others were in corners with their backs to the room, a few were in the hall outside, and a group was clustered around my desk talking. She finally located her son crouched under a table, absorbed in some work. I tried to explain that to me, this was a genuinely disciplined classroom. As long as there was a purpose in all the activity, as long as no one interfered with the purpose of anyone else, regimentation and control from above were unnecessary. The basis of true discipline is respect for the rights of others, the ability to set goals for oneself, the ability to collaborate with others, and, most important, the exercise of self-control and the will to subordinate when necessary, one's own immediate needs to the overall needs of the group.

These are difficult skills—difficult to learn and difficult to teach. It is much easier to organize a classroom along traditional lines of strictly imposed discipline than to give direction to a roomful of individuals, all intent on "doing their own thing." It is even more difficult to establish the kind of order in which I believe in a classroom such as mine, with children from such widely different backgrounds.

The children from middle-class families, for the most part, are used to being persuaded to follow directions from an adult. Their parents are willing to take the time to explain their rulings and are ready to answer questions about them. These children expect me to show them what they can and cannot do and they tend to argue about the amount of freedom that should be allowed in the classroom; only in rare cases, however, are they immediately willing and able to go through the difficult and painful process of learning *self*-control.

Black children often find it even more difficult to understand and handle my approach. Most of them are expected to "snap to it" on command at home; any attempt to argue or even any hesitation is met with instant reprisal. Small wonder then, that they are ready to explode when they come to school —it is the only place where they can give vent to their rebellious feelings. When they come into a classroom such as mine, they are at first unable to deal with the freedom I offer—it is too sharp a contrast with the discipline at home. They tend to interpret my approach as weakness and will attempt to defy any rule. Often it takes a long time before they can be brought to realize that freedom in the classroom does not mean that "anything goes."

I start laying the basis for self-discipline in my class by creating an atmosphere of mutual trust and respect between teacher and students. The children must be made to feel that we are all equally involved in the life of the class, that we are working together, and that we must help each other to reach a common goal.

From the beginning, I made a point of not setting myself apart from the children. True, I am the adult in charge, but I demand respect from my students not because of my position as their teacher, but because I am an individual in my own right, with needs and interests that have to be considered. This means that I must appear to my students not as a symbol of authority, but as a real person, an individual with his good points and his weaknesses. I let them discuss and criticize everything about me—my appearance, my possessions, my personal habits, my likes and dislikes—nothing is sacrosanct. My big "Jewish" nose has been the target of jokes in every class I ever had; my clothes, my car, my vacation plans are all objects for comment and discussions. The children use this familiarity to establish the fact that they have a personal relationship with me. Annabelle, a small and very lively black girl, once brought the house down when she looked at me thoughtfully and finally pronounced, "Mr. D., you are a nice man—but UGLEE!" Every year the children discuss when I will get married and pick suitable candidates for me from among the unmarried teachers. Dick even gave me detailed instructions on how to welcome my girl friend when she comes to see me. I was to lean out of the window, champagne glass in hand (full, of course), and call out "Come up baby, I have just finished reading *Playboy* magazine."

For my part I try to make the children feel that I recognize their needs and interests and feel bound to consider them. I show them that I am interested in them as people, not only as students. I comment on the girls' hairstyles and on their clothes, I let the boys tell me about their hobbies, I enter into their concerns about sports. If the kids are free to comment on and make fun of my pursuits, I am equally free to do the same about theirs. A free and easy relationship is soon established with most of the children in each class.

I cannot, of course, relate equally well to all children. There will always be special sympathies and antipathies, and the children will soon recognize that fact and must learn to live with it. I have my preferences, just as they have theirs; I have my moods and my personal problems; I become tired and I become angry—all these reactions are my prerogative as a human being. But all children should feel that I always try to see the other person's point of view and that I try to be as fair as possible. When I make a mistake, they are free to point it out, and I will not hesitate to acknowledge the fact that I can see that I was wrong. As a result, I often have to deal with complaints such as these:

> I wish to issue a complaint on your prejudice views on children in our class. I am not only giving you my views but also those who sit with me and those who are around the room.

Alan M. did build up a reputation of getting up when not necessary but you now yell at him for things like sharpening a pencil, giving back borrowed items, or returning a pair of scissors or crayons, or a ruler. I think you should take into consideration the possibility of him getting up when it is necessary.

Byron you pick on most and pick out every little bad thing he does. You ambarress him and make an example of him almost every chance you get.

I would suggest that you now take a little more into consideration the situation of the class might improve. You also might get more respect from people in the class.

Your critic,
P.B.

Or:

Mr. D. gave me an impression of being a pretty good guy at the beginning of the year. I didn't mind his picking on me. just as long as I could get a crack back to him.

In the middle of the year he began to show signs of a dictator. He began to take people out of various events and office for just (as it looked) the fun of it . . .

And another:

I think you are a bad and good teacher. You give us a lot of freedom, but you, when you do punish, punish to harshly. I think you know the rest about you (what I like and hate).

Those who cope best with my approach are the children who have a sense of self-respect and a feeling of security. Bobby caught on right away and immediately began to joke back and forth with me freely, yet showing all the while that he sincerely respected me as an individual. Sue, although she was very shy at first, soon began to feel quite at home and no longer hesitated to show me and the class her thoughts, feelings, and her personality. It is very gratifying when children respond so well and really appreciate what I am trying to do.

One letter I received at the end of the school year commented:

> I thought you were the best teacher in the grade this
> year. You tried to understand how we felt and why
> we felt that way. You tried to help us when we had
> problems. You would let us joke for a few minutes
> when we were in a good mood. When we were having
> a discussion, you tried not to bring your own ideas
> into it.

Perhaps the most striking and unusual reaction was
Richard's. He came to school determined to fight me as he
had fought every other teacher he had had in school. His
mother told me that he came home after his first day in class
and gave vent to his feelings of relief at the atmosphere I had
tried to set. Asked what his new teacher was like, he gave a
deep sigh, "Oh, he's nice!" he said.

Self-discipline is not something that can easily be learned
in the span of one year in school. Many children can feel the
freedom I offer but are unable to take advantage of it. Instead,
they long for more "real" discipline:

> I think you would be a perfect teacher if you would
> be a little stricter. I know you don't want to teach any
> different than you are now, but for different classes you
> have to teach differently. Last years class might have
> done good work this way, but we don't! . . .

Some become a little frightened that order will break down in
my system:

> I think the freedom you give is a good idea, and so
> is the fact that you can laugh at yourself with the class.
> Sometimes though, things get out of hand and you have
> trouble maintaining order. I know that some teachers
> can give freedom *and* keep control. I think you should
> try to acheiv this. . . .

Some children take the balanced view. I quote in full a letter

received from a student evaluating my performance for the
year:

> Dear Mr. D.
> You are a swell teacher and hope you stay that way
> except for a few things like have too many pets etc.
> But in years to come you will find that many people
> will begin to like you except for a few. Next year I
> hope I'll remember something you told this year. That's
> all I have to say. remember me always.
>
> E.
> P.S. I'm forgetful.

The children who have the most difficulty with my kind of
discipline are those who have either too little or too much
self-control.

Byron, Steve, and Bill were all used to having their own
way. None could feel at ease in the classroom atmosphere
that combined freedom with the demand for self-discipline.
All of them fought me every inch of the way, constantly testing whether any real limits would be drawn for them. Byron's
problem was aggravated by his overpowering need to gain the
approval of his peers, which made it almost mandatory for
him to "go overboard" in his behavior. In the class of a strict
disciplinarian the year before, Byron had presented no problem—he had adapted to the teacher's view of what he should
be. With me he was being himself and he was trying to work
something out for himself.

It is difficult, but not impossible to teach such children
self-discipline, and when they begin to learn, it is very reward-
ing. For example, Bill one day brought a tape recorder to
school and began to play with it in class. When I asked him
to put it away, he refused outright; when I insisted, he
threatened to leave the classroom: "Go ahead," I replied. "If
you can't work with other people and respect them but have
to do exactly as you like, you had better leave." He gave me
a surprised look but got up and walked out of the door. A

few minutes later he was back, facing me with some embarrassment. "I just came back to tell you that I know I was wrong," he apologized. I smiled at him as he sat down; Bill was learning to set limits for himself.

Bill was one case also where the therapy approach to the distribution of responsible jobs paid off. The kids decided to put on a play in class, and we were looking for a director. I gave the job to Bill, curious to see how he would handle it. It turned out that this boy, who had been incapable of sustaining an organized effort before, took his assignment very seriously. He saw to it that everyone followed directions and became very annoyed when he found some children to be unreliable in following his directions. It was interesting for me to see that the children for the most part were ready to listen to and obey Bill in this instance, even though he had made himself so unpopular before. The experience proved to be a good exercise in self-discipline for Bill.

If I had difficulties with many of the white kids, the problem was even more acute with the black students. It takes much more time and energy to establish the right kind of atmosphere with the ghetto children. All of them are on the defensive with a white teacher, always on the alert for signs of racial prejudice. None expect to be trusted or to be accepted for what they are. And yet they need so badly to feel trusted and accepted! Conversely, most of them find it difficult to develop genuine respect for and trust in a white teacher.

Once they grasp the idea that I am genuinely trying to establish a personal relationship with them, they will often "throw the book" at me in an attempt to find out whether this really applies to them as they are. Brad, for example, would challenge me by using the most obscene language he knew. It was as if he were saying to me, "This is the kind of person I am. Do you still say that you accept and respect me?" It was only when I refused to be shocked that he began to believe that he was a real person in my eyes.

Physical contact is very important to ghetto children. They

come from a culture where this way of communication is used much more widely than among the white middle class. So I do not hesitate to put my hand on Brad's shoulder or to pull Marva's braids when she teases me about my nose. The physical contact, *if it stems from genuine feeling,* is warmth and reassurance and a reaffirmation to them that I know and am glad that they are there.

Even in an angry confrontation, physical measures can be valuable. Ghetto children expect adults to react this way and will respond to this more easily and readily than to verbal commands.

This was brought home to me in the case of Dan. Dan was typically one of "those kids" when he began the school year in my class. He was a tough little boy, handsome and full of charm but extremely difficult to deal with. He was one of the most unmanageable kids in the class. He would constantly talk back, argue, disrupt the class, and start fights with other children. Although he was shorter than most, he was strong and wiry and could take on almost any boy in the group. His battle cry against any attempt to restrain him was, "I know why you are doing it—you're prejudiced!" He was one of the children I periodically had to send down to the principal's office, and one day he even had to be in-school suspended.

It was his very defiance of any kind of authority that paved the way for getting through to Dan. We had had a very difficult day in school, with Dan making life so impossible for me and for the other children, that I finally lost my temper and grabbed him by the arm in an access of rage. Immediately afterwards I felt very bad, since I really do not believe in physical punishment or coercion as an assertion of authority.

I had long wanted to get in touch with Dan's family, and this incident gave me the final impetus. I decided to go visit them, explain the situation, and ask for their help.

Dan lived with his grandmother in a small apartment in the projects. She was willing to hear me but had very little to say herself. In the middle of the interview, however, Dan's uncle came in. He was a leader in the black community who proved very interested in Dan's progress. He asked me to let him know next time Dan was in trouble, rather than trying to deal with him alone. I took this to mean "Don't touch him again!" I found out later that he had first inquired about me to know whether I could be trusted.

Dan sat throughout the interview without saying a single word. Although I had told him I was coming, he seemed surprised when I actually appeared. But somehow, the incident proved to be the starting point of a good relationship between him and me. I think that I had proven to him that I was a real person with real feelings by the very fact that I had grabbed hold of him and shown my anger; the physical restraint of middle-class teachers who refrain from any tangible show of anger often puzzles black children. Or maybe it was the interest I had shown in him by coming to see his family. Whatever it was, Dan now began to respond to me. In spite of the fact that he was failing every subject so far, there had never been any doubt in my mind that Dan was a very intelligent boy. One has only to look at his eyes—bright, sparkling, and alive—to see that this was true. His rare smile, when it came, lit up his whole face and brought out two dimples, allowing a glimpse of the lively, keen wit behind the tough facade.

Once the ice was broken between us, I could work with Dan, and he soon began to show some success in math. As soon as he felt that he could become involved in the academic part of the school, his behavior began to improve. Suddenly, he was no longer the ringleader in disrupting his math group; instead he was asking the children to be quiet so that he could do some work. He welcomed the news that a school volunteer would come in to tutor him and settled down to work with her without a single attempt at fighting the new "teacher." So serious was he about his math, that he asked for tutoring during Easter vacation so that he would not fall behind.

Dan still got into trouble in school—miracles don't happen—but he seemed more willing to see the rights and wrongs of a situation. One day he came running out of the art room ten minutes early, furious. He had been asked to clean up the tables, while the other children were washing the sinks. "I don't have to clean up for everyone else." This was the old Dan talking. "How come she picked me?" I made him go back. "If you don't want to clean the tables, try and get someone else to do it and wash the sink for him," I suggested. "Everyone has to help to clean up somehow." The old Dan would not have listened but would have gone on shouting. This one had learned to stop himself and consider. Yes, he decided, he could see that he could not be the only one not to help. He gave me a quick smile and went back.

The best moment in my developing relationship with Dan came when I saw the first signs that he was learning *self-discipline*. He was in a group of children who all got into trouble with me. Instead of doing the math work I had assigned for the period, they had been fooling around, and when it came time to go to the playground, none of the work had been done. I told the whole group that they would have to stay inside and finish the work for which they had been responsible.

Dan was furious. While the others resigned themselves and settled down to the work, he screamed that he wouldn't do it, he wouldn't sit down, and he refused to follow directions. I told him that I would hold him responsible for the work and went to the playground with the rest of the class. When I came back, I found that Dan had defied my ruling—the work was not done. I said nothing but collected the assignments from the others.

Next morning when the class assembled, Dan was one of the first children at my desk. Without a word, he laid in front of me the completed assignment, beautifully done and all correct. He had worked things out for himself and decided that he had to comply with a legitimate demand!

Incidents like these reinforce rather than weaken a relationship between teacher and student. Dan did the homework basically because he trusted me and liked me and valued my opinion of him. These feelings allowed him to think about an issue without being blinded by fear, hate, and the need for self-defense. Every so often he felt the need to reassert the relationship with me. He would come up and just stand with his hand on my shoulder while I talked to other children, sometimes for as long as five minutes at a time. He continued to be unruly in class, but much of this behavior now stemmed from the fact that he wanted my attention and felt that the other children were receiving too much of it. He found it hard to take when I talked to the class as a whole; he would refuse to take the seat assigned to him, wander around to pick another, refuse to take that one, interrupt my talk—all attempts to draw my attention away from the others and make me focus on him. But he was giving up his fight against me as a representative of the school.

Some children, on the other hand, are problems because they are *too* controlled. This is not self-discipline but fear. One such case was Graham. Graham first attracted my notice because he was too disciplined. A good-looking, well-dressed black boy, he sat quietly at his desk throughout the school day. He was silent and well-behaved, keeping his close-cropped head down, and his eyes carefully lowered. What caught my attention was a sense of his utter remoteness. He seemed completely withdrawn from the life of the class around him. If he caused no disturbance, he also did not participate in any activity. He had no friends, and he hardly ever spoke to anyone. The tight control he kept over himself showed up even in his handwriting. It was cramped and almost illegible, squeezed up at the very top of the page, eloquent evidence that Graham was giving away nothing of himself.

I discovered that, although he did little or no school work, he had an outstanding artistic talent. Throughout most of the school day, he would sit and draw beautifully executed, strictly accurate little pictures that showed great ability and promise. But his drawings, like his handwriting, were frightening in their constraint. I felt strongly that such talent should not be allowed to go to waste, but how could he ever become a good artist if it was impossible for him to communicate anything of *himself* to the outside world?

I began to find out about Graham. It was with some surprise that I learned that two years earlier he had been a considerable discipline problem. He had started the integrated program in the fourth grade. He and a group of his classmates had been assigned to another elementary school in the city. He had proved so uncontrollable in his new surroundings that he had to be taken out in the middle of the second year. It was then he came to my school.

Thrust abruptly into a strange environment and cut off from his friends, he did not dare defy his new teacher. Instead, he chose to withdraw into an impenetrable shell. School became an alien world, and he took no interest in anything that went on there. Anxious not to attract attention, he did as little work as possible and hardly ever spoke. He trusted no one, made no friends, and felt that he could expect nothing. His only outlet during this year was his art. His teacher the previous year had recognized his talent and was so impressed that she arranged for him to be admitted to an art school in the neighborhood.

The problem clearly for me was to get him to produce in other areas and to teach him to communicate in some way. But I was at a loss on how to reach him. When I spoke to him, he heard but did not listen, and he did not react at all. Most attempts by the other pupils to approach him he met with hostility or indifference. Contact with him would have to be established in some other, less direct way.

I began by repeatedly praising his art work. This, I hoped, would help to break down the wall of distrust he had erected between us. Here, he knew he could believe what I was telling him; he knew that he was good, and he was proud of it. Over and over again, I told him that he could also be successful in other areas. Then I discovered that he also had an aptitude for math. Here, I thought, was something to build on. This was an area that required no self-expression on his part and thus might feel "safe" to him. There was a good chance that here he could be persuaded to achieve some success.

I began to give him special work to do. At every forward step, I pointed out his achievement to him and encouraged him to try a little harder and a little longer with the next one. It was at this point that Bobby intervened by offering to help him. Slowly, he began to do some real work in school, and slowly he began to trust me and to listen to me.

What I discovered about his family background went far towards explaining Graham's personality and his problems. His father's strict discipline explained his inability to communicate verbally. His father would not allow any of his children to speak at all during dinner, and after dinner they had to keep as quiet as possible whenever he was home. He also had extremely rigid ideas about obedience. When his commands were not obeyed, punishment was swift and rigorous. The children might easily find themselves locked out of the apartment for the night, if they were not home on time.

Once I had established some kind of contact with Graham, I asked his mother for permission to work with him after school. Ostensibly I came to work with him on his math, and his performance in this area improved. But my main purpose during these tutoring sessions was to show Graham that I was really interested in him and cared about what he did. What he needed was a feeling that there was one adult in school whom he could trust, who was concerned, and to whom he could turn.

With his growing sense of achievement, a gradual change came over Graham. He was beginning to find his feet. No longer did he sit quietly at his seat, head and eyes lowered. Now he was constantly interrupting the class and creating a disturbance. He selected Charlene as a natural target and began to cater to her desire to be at the center of attention. He would get up to get a drink of water and hit her in passing, or he would call out some remark across the room to her, which would make the class laugh and disrupt the work. Outside the classroom, he became more and more aggressive. He refused to follow school rules, started fights on the playground, and was rude to the teachers who tried to restrain him. To those who knew of his previous record, he seemed simply to have reverted to type. "An uncontrollable boy," was the verdict at faculty meetings. "He needs a strong hand to keep him in line." The implication was that I could not or would not provide the necessary discipline.

But I knew that a strong hand only made Graham resentful and angry. One day I came upon him in the hall, held tightly in the grip of another teacher. I intervened and took him back to the classroom. He was tense with rage and in tears with a sense of injustice and outrage. He had been only one in a group of boys who had been running down the hall, but the teacher had unhesitatingly singled *him* out for disciplining. Not only that, but the teacher had handled him so roughly that some of the buttons had come off his shirt. It felt like an attack on his dignity as an individual and as a human being. Above all, it was the unfairness that rankled. "I wasn't the only one," he said again and again. "Why didn't he grab one of the other boys." I agreed with him that the other boys should have been punished too, but I also tried to make him see that he was to blame even if many others had been involved.

The important thing, it seemed to me, was not enforcing the rules and preserving order at any cost. If we have controlled the behavior of an "uncontrollable" boy, we have not really done anything at all. Graham who sits quietly at his desk, stifling all his talent is, in my view, no more a useful member of society than Charlene who acknowledges no control and disrupts the class.

What I tried to teach Graham was that there was security and justice for him in the school world. My problem was to encourage him to come out of his self-inflicted isolation, while at the same time teaching him that he could assert himself and be accepted without resorting to acts that could not be tolerated by the society in which he had to live. What was happening to Graham was that he was coming back to life. For the first time in the new school, he was yielding to his need to take part in what was going on and to be accepted by other children his own age. After the period of tight and unnatural control he had imposed upon himself, the only way he could find to break out of his shell was by extreme and violent action.

This method proved doubly effective for his purpose. Since his difficulties with Bobby, the only group of children to whom he felt he could appeal for acceptance and admiration were the black kids. These boys, under Jason's leadership, admired tough and aggressive behavior, and many had become notorious for their wild exploits. Graham felt that he had to imitate Jason or team up with him in order to become one of the "in" group.

There were some positive aspects to this new Graham. He had come out of his isolation and was making contact with other people. This made it easier for him to listen to me and to think about what I was trying to tell him, but it was clearly impossible to let him persist in flouting the rules of the school.

Perhaps his most painful lesson in this respect was learned on the occasion of a class trip to a nearby art museum. This outing had been planned for a long time. Graham had been looking forward to it, and because of his talent I particularly wanted him to have this experience. However, I had had to warn him repeatedly that I could not let him go if he went on breaking the rules and getting into trouble. Only the day before the trip, he started a fight on the playground. I told him that this was his last chance. If anything else happened, he would not be allowed to go tomorrow. He knew very well that I wanted him to go, and he may have thought that I didn't mean it. The next day the class was getting ready to board the bus and the line was forming by the door, when Graham began hitting the boy ahead of him. He probably thought that he was safe and that no one would be kept back from the trip at this late date. I felt I had no choice. Although I hated to do it, I told him that he would have to stay in the school while the others went without him.

This was only one incident in many. Often I felt that it was an uphill fight, but by the end of the year I began to see some success. Graham was learning self-control and responsibility. He had had a problem with money all year. Repeatedly he had borrowed lunch money from the office and had neglected to pay it back. On several occasions, his name was read out over the public address system with a list of students who owed the school money. On one occasion I happened to know that he had come to school with four dollars in his pocket to pay for a class excursion. I told him that I would take one dollar of that money to pay the office what he owed, and would lend him a dollar of my own money to make up the difference. He now owed me instead of the office, and I told him I expected to be paid back as soon as possible. Two weeks later, without having to be reminded, Graham paid me back.

The day before the end of the school year, the same thing happened. The public address system announced that Graham owed the school money. This time he came to me first to ask that I lend him the sum so that he could pay his debts to the school. He made a date at school with me for the day after school closed and promised that he would bring the money then. Unfortunately, I was unavoidably detained and did not reach school until two hours after I was to meet Graham. I heard that he had kept the appointment and had waited a whole hour before giving up. I was pleased that he had come and convinced that I would have to write off the money he owed me. But the next day he was back again, although he could not know whether or not I would be there.

Self-discipline can begin only after children learn to look

at themselves—indeed, the painful progress of self-knowledge is part of the art of self-discipline. Byron, Graham, and Dan all first had to be persuaded to give up the facades they had developed to deal with the "system." Once they throw off their token submission to control from above and without, they will show their true personalities. The immediate results can be disconcerting. Graham was certainly more manageable before he lost his armor. Byron and Dan reacted to the sudden loss of stringent rules with uncontrolled and disruptive behavior. But once children feel that they are genuinely trusted and respected, they can be reached and the growth process can begin. It is then that they must again and again be confronted with their own behavior and given the opportunity to decide what to do about it. Graham was given "enough rope to hang himself" and then left to handle the situations that came up. If he could not control himself within the limits he knew existed, he had to take the consequences. Bill had to experience for himself time and time again that he could not with impunity disregard the rights of others. Only when he began to understand what he was doing, could he begin to try and modify his behavior.

It is my conviction that in an integrated classroom this is the only approach to discipline that can work. Only this concept allows children to retain their self-respect and their feeling of identity, while teaching them to respect the rights of others and to conform to the rules of an ordered society.

TEACHING AN
INTEGRATED CLASSROOM

When children feel that they are respected as individuals and that it is safe to be what they are, one can begin to teach them, and they will begin to learn. Unlike the need for self-control, which has to be painstakingly developed, the need to know is there—all teachers have to do, it would seem, is to encourage it.

All too often, unfortunately, the school does just the opposite. Children come to kindergarten full of the curiosity and the desire to know that is natural to this age, bubbling with life and the eagerness to experience new things. The classroom, from then on, is their proving ground. This is where they spend the greater part of their day and the greater part of their year. This is where they find out about the world in which they live, where they test themselves in the eyes of their peers, where they learn to live outside their family circle. Here they find out every day how they look to others, whether they are successful, and how they can be accepted. Here they acquire the knowledge that they will need for their future lives.

Many of these needs and expectations clash with the demands of the school. While children are wholly involved in shaping their lives and personalities, the school expects them to concentrate on one goal only—absorbing the material the teacher is told to teach. Different children learn in different ways: one will learn fast, another slowly; one will be good at social studies, another at math; one will work better before lunch, another after. Moreover, children do not interrupt other aspects of their lives while they are listening to the teacher: some will be preoccupied in gaining the approval of their friends, others in protecting themselves from real or imagined threats to their personality; some may be daydreaming, others thinking of their after-school plans. Yet, we assemble them all in one room together and present all of them with the same subject matter at the same time. Teaching has been defined as the transfer of knowledge intact from one mind to another—from a teacher or from a book to a child—and we assume that the information the teacher imparts must mean the same thing to children as it does to adults, the same thing to Johnnie as it does to Mary. "The teacher," said one boy to me resentfully "*gives* us the opinions he wants us to have."

We assume that all children of the same age group can be asked to absorb more or less the same amount of information in more or less the same period of time. We assume that the "knowledge" thus acquired can be measured in quantitative terms and that children's performance should be measured by comparing them with their peers.

In the conflict between children's individual growth needs and the demands set by the school, it is the school that almost invariably wins. Faced with a mold to which they are expected to conform, most children soon learn to "turn off" their natural curiosity. Their eagerness disappears, and interest dies down as their responses become increasingly predictable and they seek to adapt to the mode of behavior and performance that will gain them the approval of the adult world. Those who do not openly fight the system—black and white alike—learn to *hide* what is real and true and important to them at any given moment.

I knew that if I did not want this to happen in my classroom, I would have to "stop, look, and listen" before I could be successful. True learning can take place only when children feel safe. The atmosphere of freedom and mutual respect I try to set in my classroom helps as a first step—it removes the threatening factor. Sooner or later, depending on the individual, most kids feel that I am not trying to "put them down" or "give" them opinions. They come to realize that I welcome the expression of their personalities and that I look on them as people in their own right.

But this alone is not enough. Richard, who immediately felt safe with me, did not ever really begin to learn in my classroom. Deborah, Graham, and even Jason eventually recognized the fact that I was not prejudiced against them, but that did not produce academic success. The teacher's respect for a child is a prerequisite, rather than a spur, to learning.

Children will learn in response to some need. This does not necessarily have to be the need to know—it can stem from any one of a number of sources. I felt that my first task as a teacher was to listen to my children and observe them to find, if possible, the key in every individual that will stimulate learning. If I could find out about every student's basic concerns and interests and respond to these in some way, if I could make them feel that their thoughts and opinions were valuable—to me as well as to themselves—if I could let them *live* while they are in school, then I might be able to help them learn.

Easiest for me are those children who have focussed on a particular interest or who bring to school a genuine desire to learn. Charlie, for example, went to the library to choose a book and came back with a volume on the Pueblo Indians. From this he began to develop a consuming interest in archaeology and anthropology. All I had to do was to allow him to pursue this. He did his science report on archaeology, and I structured his reading program around his new hobby. From that time on, Charlie could be largely left to his own devices; his interest provided most of the direction he needed in his school work.

Sue came from a family where everyone was deeply involved with intellectual concerns. Stimulated by the atmosphere in her home, she came to school with a real desire to learn, which stemmed from the conviction that ideas were important and that learning was fun.

Cases such as these are all too rare. It is more usual to find children who will be very ready to work in the expectation of the rewards the educational system offers to those who can achieve. These are the children who have always been successful in school and who have learned to use this method to gain the approval of their parents and teachers.

Tommy, for example, was almost always concerned with finding out whether the work he was asked to do would be graded. If he could not expect to garner an A, he was not really interested in making an effort. Byron, in spite of his difficulties with his social life, maintained a consistently high performance in academic work. His reward was the approval of the adult world, his improved image of himself, and his realization—shared by many in the class—that he was "making it."

Problems can arise with students who work hard in the expectation of tangible rewards, when the effort does not bring the expected result. John was one of those who had always succeeded in school. But for John it was not enough to succeed; he was driven by a relentless ambition to be *the* best and to be always first. It was inevitable that sooner or later he would be beaten by someone. At the end of his year in my class he suffered a tremendous disappointment. In the annual award-giving ceremony of the school, he was passed over in favor of another boy, who won the coveted letter of the school.

John found it very difficult to cope with this defeat. It was almost as if it threatened him with personal destruction. I saw his distress and sat down with him after school for a long talk. I tried to make him realize that he really had not lost anything, that his work was just as good as he had thought, and that it really did not matter who was first. Next day I found a letter from him on my desk:

> Dear Mr. D.
>
> I know you well enough as a person and a teacher to be able to write this letter too.
>
> After you gave me that talk yesterday, I realized something. The "R" is a material object. Probably the main reason I was so upset was because this award was so built up. I was so worried about what other people would think of me since I wouldn't get the "R". I also

realized that you knew I was disturbed and I thank you for your time which you didn't have to give.

I was too worried about other people. It's good to worry about other people, but it's not good to worry about what other people will think of you.

I have proved myself to my classmates and you. (I hope.) You know what my worth is (In $ and ¢).

This year taught me many many things (among other things) It also taught me how to lose, or I should say you taught me that.

The "R" or not, it was a great year for me (I hope for you) and as you wished me, I wish you

"All Future Luck"

> Yours sincerely, your friend and student
> John

"Among other things," John was learning to look at himself and reevaluate what was truly important to him. He may have still been thinking in terms of "$ and ¢," but he was also trying to work out new values. John was growing up, and growing up is hard work. As a teacher, all I could do was try and help him when things became difficult.

Tommy and John were not my real problems. These boys were reasonably assured of success if they continued as they were doing. Tommy, if he wanted them, would go on receiving A's, and John was likely to win many of the awards offered. Both boys were almost certain to attain their long-term goals: a good college and achieving successful careers in their professions. In spite of occasional setbacks, they would both continue to feel strong and "on top of things."

My real difficulties lay with the children who did not believe that they could succeed and who were so afraid of failure that they could not even begin to try.

Richard was one of these. Although he was no longer afraid of me as a teacher, he still was completely convinced that he could not perform, and he was terribly afraid that he would expose his weakness by trying. Throughout his stay in school, Richard never felt strong or "on top" of anything. He also desperately needed the approval and acceptance of the other children. This might have been the key to his success; unfortunately, the opportunity to use it came too late in the school year. The class had decided to put on a play. In the tryouts for the lead part, Richard showed unexpected strength —no one had known that he had any acting talent. Impressed, the children elected him for the part. I now watched him, for the first time since I had known him, make a strenuous and sustained effort. He worked hard on his lines and gave a very good performance. I could have tried to use this success to spur him on to try in other fields, but there was no time left— graduation for the sixth grade came just a few weeks after the play. Richard left, however, with some sense of achievement and a new feeling of safety. He made this speech in class at the end of school:

> I think that graduation is more than a ceremony. It is the end of a long period of time in which you have proved to yourself that you have actually accomplished something. This need not be one plus one is two, or two plus two is four, etc. . . . but perhaps you have found a philosophy. Perhaps of teaching, perhaps of playing baseball. I have found a philosophy of teaching. This is letting the pupils find the information and not you forcing it down his throat. I believe that if you get your own information you actually absorb it. If it *is* forced down your throat you are bored to tears, so you reject it.
>
> Mr. D's philosophy as I understand it is the following. The student must have freedom to find the information after being inspired. He believes that the teacher student relations should be improved and as a result he changed them. This was done joking with the pupils and not maintaining a tense atmosphere so tense the pupils can't think about anything else but getting out of here. I feel this is very necessary especially in the sixth grade. . . .
>
> Let me dwell a bit on the importance of this philosophy. First off it helps you gain confidence. Secondly,

it helps you to work and last but not least the teacher helps you understand you problems. All of these help you to work more efficiently. Why? because your problems affect your work. . . .

In closing, I would like to thank Mr. D'Amore for proving to me that I can do it and for proving that my philosophy works.

Most of the problems I came up against in school were pointed up with particular force by the black children. Whatever the personal difficulties they may have had, they had to contend in addition with the problems they faced as a group. Many of the ghetto children assumed from the beginning that they were dumber than the white children and could never successfully compete with them. Brad and Graham were both bright and able boys but both had to be urged over and over again to try. When I asked them outright whether they thought it would be useless, both admitted that they thought this was the case—white children were so much smarter anyway. Deborah told the class with her customary courage: "When I first came to this school, I was sure that all white kids and all white people were smart." For her it worked out a little better than for the two boys. "I've found at least one since," she went on, to the laughter of the entire class, "who is dumber than I am."

Verna expressed her admiration for the smart and successful student in an unusual poem:

THE SMART CHILD

The smart child, big, beautiful and wild
The smart child, big, nice and swift
Beautiful
He full with an education
Nice
Thoughtful of others to learn
Swift
He's the only one who does his homework
The smart child, big, beautiful and wild
Beautiful

Verna herself, although very bright, is not doing well in school; she has to contend with too many emotional problems.

These attitudes were unfortunately reinforced by some inescapable facts of life. For reasons intimately connected with ghetto conditions most of the black children, by the time they have been in school a few years, are considerably behind the middle-class students in the level of skills expected in their grade. The results are reflected in the class groupings, and the children all realize this, no matter how much the teacher tries to disguise them. My school groups children according to ability in reading; one third-grade teacher named her reading groups after colors in an attempt to take all the stigma out of the procedure. The children, however, believe in calling a spade a spade. "Mummy," asked one white girl in the class, "why doesn't the teacher call the purple group the bus group? They are the same kids." "When the bell rings," said Deborah bitterly, "the black kids go off to the idiot classes." The result of this situation is that very soon both teachers and children expect black kids to perform badly.

A child who is confronted daily with evidence that he is a failure and whose teacher *expects* him to fail will soon give up trying. Many of the black children are so firmly convinced that they can never do anything right that they will not even attempt the simplest tasks. Self-direction and independent work become a psychological impossibility. Greg, a very bright and able boy, refused to open his math book unless I sat down next to him and asked him to do so. Once he had been persuaded to find the right page, he had to be led step by step through the exercises. He did not have the slightest difficulty with the work—in fact, he was one of the brightest children in the group—but he didn't know it, and he couldn't believe it when I told him.

Ruthie was another such case. Also capable, she too had to be led through the steps of an assignment. When I asked the class to write a composition, Ruthie would sit idle while most of the others began to write. "I don't understand," she would say. When I explained the topic to her again, she would write one sentence, then come up to my desk and ask: "Is this good?" Again and again she would have to be reassured that she was doing all right before she could proceed.

Marva, who was doing quite well academically, was convinced that she could never pass. She insisted on being transferred into a lower group, where she could feel safer. Only after the first test had shown her that she could manage a passing grade, did she consent to give the higher group another try.

Black children are further handicapped by the fact that they come from a culture that does not emphasize listening. "Take out your math books," I would say, and the black children would not react. Only when they see the others act, do they ask what they are expected to do. I may have to repeat the directions several times before they are followed. This can be extremely exasperating to a teacher. It took me a long time to realize that these students were not fighting me—they simply had not heard.

Life in school becomes particularly difficult for black children who have the ability but not the necessary skills to keep up with the class. Dick, for instance, was a boy with a truly exceptional feeling and sensitivity for words. His vocabulary was far in advance of his age, and he knew how to use his imagination and the words he had learned to make up original and very touching stories. But the stories had to be told for Dick could not write, read, or spell properly; so most of his remarkable talent was going to waste. Instead of using his gift, he had to sit in class, idle and bored; it is not surprising that he became a discipline problem, constantly in trouble with the authorities.

Children such as these will learn as soon as they feel that there is someone who is truly concerned about them and who believes in them and wants them to succeed. Dan, who started the year as a tight ball of defense, was so alert for any sign of racial prejudice and so preoccupied with fighting off the potential enemy that he could not perform academically. But once I had established contact with him, he began to work, and success in school became important to him. I became aware *how* important it was to him one day when the school was expecting a guest speaker to address the fifth and sixth grades. His visit had been discussed, and his topic, drug addiction, was of urgent interest to the children. The two grades assembled in one room to hear him; he proved to be an excellent speaker, and the children were spellbound. In the middle of the lecture I looked around the rapt faces and suddenly realized that Dan was missing. I went looking for him and found him in his own classroom, bent in complete absorption over a page of math exercises. He had finally caught on to multiplication and felt he couldn't leave it to listen to the speaker!

Ted's case too was striking. He was a big, strong boy, too old for fifth grade, with a reputation for violent and aggressive behavior similar to Jason's. He was bright and could be very appealing, with a lively sense of humor and an ability to laugh at himself, but he felt humiliated by his lack of success in school—he had been held back twice and did not have some of the basic skills—and wouldn't work. Instead he spent most of his time in school fighting the other boys. I decided to try a one-to-one tutoring arrangement for him, and a school volunteer was found who came in once a week to work with him in math. For weeks the volunteer and Ted spent time together without accomplishing any work. His attention span was very short; he couldn't manage to sit still at all. He would open and close desk drawers, fidget with his comb, pull his shirt up to his neck, push his chair around the room—anything to keep moving. Nevertheless, Ted and the tutor got on well together, and a sincere liking sprang up between them. Ted began to make halfhearted attempts at learning the multiplication tables, more to convince the volunteer that she was useful than to learn math. Whenever he could, to prove how smart he was—Ted had a great desire to show that he was smart— he would cheat by looking at the answers in the book or on the back of flashcards. When caught, he would always concede defeat with a charming smile.

The relationship came to mean something. One day Ted greeted the volunteer by saying, "Larry (his best friend, but a boy completely unknown to the tutor) said you weren't coming today." What he was really saying was, "This is important to me. Can I really rely on your coming?" In answer, the volunteer offered to come twice a week, and Ted enthusiastically accepted. Three weeks later, he asked her to come every day. But still, only the most desultory work was going on in the sessions, and no progress could be seen at all.

Then one day, without any visible reason, Ted came to his tutoring session with a book of multiplication exercises, sat down, and began to work. The boy who could not remember the eight-times did multiplication with three numbers, and there was no mistake in the first example. He went on to the next one—correct. Both he and the tutor began to work in mounting excitement. Each one did the examples on separate sheets of paper, and the results were compared—correct every time! After half an hour of happy competition, the tutor reminded Ted that it was time for him to go back to the classroom—no session had ever lasted more than 25 minutes. "I'm not going to stop now," he said, absorbed, not even looking up. He stayed for a whole hour, concentrating on his work as he had never done before, and at the end of the hour he had finished the whole page without making a single mistake! Glowing with pride—who could say that he wasn't smart now?—he came back to the classroom to show me what he had done. For days afterwards Larry's life was made miserable by Ted's boasting at every turn of his academic prowess. The transformation was not permanent of course. Ted was still a problem in the classroom when he had to compete with other children, and his euphoric mood did not last; neither did all other skills develop overnight. But it does prove that a child will produce when he feels that he is liked and respected and that someone really cares.

The person who shows concern and who awakens the desire to learn need not necessarily be an adult or a teacher. Some children begin to perform when they work with other children.

Graham and Bobby were one example; Jimmy and Ben were another. While Bobby was a good student who volunteered to help one who lagged behind, Ben and Jimmie were almost equally lacking in skills. Ben, a white boy, was somewhat better at reading than Jimmie, but not much. Both were somewhat immature and not well accepted by the rest of the class. They took a liking to each other and asked to be allowed to work together. As a result both improved in their work. They would sit together in a corner and work until they were tired. The rest of the time, if the class was still busy, they would fill in with quiet games or talk. The relationship made both boys feel good.

Difficult as it is to deal with an unsatisfactory self-image and a lack of skills, it is even harder to cut through the emotions that beset black children and are rooted in the facts of black life in America. Not only do they feel threatened by the school, they must also contend with a burden largely unknown to white children. Many of them are imbued with the deep anger and frustration that pervades the black community as a whole, and this may blind them to anything else.

Take Luke, for example. Luke is a bundle of mindless rage. Thin and slight, he sits quietly in his seat, seemingly withdrawn from the outside world, but his quiet is not peaceful; it is an expression of intense anger and a complete rejection of the school, a dropping out of his environment. He just sits, gathered into himself, his lower lip stuck out as far as it will go, waiting for the day to end. His anger and rage clog all his thoughts. I was startled one day by an outburst from him. We were discussing India, and I had just finished telling the class that the Hindu religion considers the cow a sacred animal and that no one is allowed to kill cows in India. Luke suddenly exploded, "If I had a cow, I would kill it *right now!*"

With Deborah, this preoccupation was more intellectualized. She could see the world only through the prism of the racial problem in America. We had spent some time discussing the history of the black people in America. We then took up a new topic—China. I told the children about the European penetration into China and of the feeling of humiliation experienced by the Chinese people. In a prewar picture of the foreign concessions in Shanghai that I passed around, a sign read, "Chinese and dogs not allowed." Here was something with which Deborah could identify. "Did the Chinese also establish an Underground Railway to escape from their masters?" she wanted to know.

Rarely, however, can black children respond like this. Too often, unfortunately, the materials used in the school reflect only the while middle-class world to which black children do not belong.

They must learn to read and write a language that is not their own. They say, "Man you smart!" They are asked to write, "You *are* smart." They say, "There ain't no . . ." and are made to write, "There are no. . . ." Their pronunciation of the English language is different from that of the middle class, but they are asked to write the middle-class version. Their language omits the final "ed" of the past tense, and they simply cannot see why they have to write it. Their vowel sounds are different from the conventional, and it is even more difficult for them to learn how to spell than for the middle-class child, because they hear the language differently. The ghetto vernacular has an entire vocabulary of its own, but the school does not recognize it as a legitimate language. Ghetto children are so often and so systematically corrected when they speak, that they often just give up altogether the attempt to express themselves. Deprived of their own language, they tend to fall behind in all other areas too. Dan, for example, had a problem with measurement calculations until I found out that he did not know that "feet" was the plural form of "foot"; he thought he had to contend with an additional measurement.

Many of the books used in school tell children of a world that does not exist. *The Little White House* (Ginn basic Readers, rev. ed., 1961), a basal reader, tells the story of a little, white family, living in a little, white house, with a white fence around it, and a garage for the family car. The white children of the family go on a vacation on a train to a farm, where they have fun with their mother and father—all unreal, even to white children (how many upper middle-class families go on vacations by train to a farm in the 1970's), but almost insulting to black children. *Around the City* (A Bank Street Reader, Macmillan Co., 1965) is clearly written with the black population in mind, but the black children described and pictured in the book are just black *faces*—in all other respects they could be white. Their hair is straight, they live in a clean city block with lots of white children and all play together in utter harmony, the police exist to help people, and parents have plenty of time to spend with them.

Textbooks used in the social studies program are equally colorless, in both senses of the word. One book tells children about the modern United States—people in big cities, it says, all live in apartments, but some live in big ones, in beautiful houses and others in old houses all crowded together. Who lives where? We are not told, and why this is so is not discussed, nor is the question even raised. Yes, there was slavery in the South before the Civil War—but what did this mean to the slaves? "The planters cared for all the needs of the slaves. Most planters treated their slaves well, although there were some who did not." (p. 206). The book mentions problems between business and labor, which quite properly rate a separate section, but the problems between the races is not mentioned. We are told what a "flapper" was and that women shingled their hair after World War I, but the riots in the big cities are not mentioned, nor is there a section about how people live in the southern states, although a section is provided for all other parts of the country. *You and the United States* (C. Samford, F. McCall, and E. F. Cunningham, Benefic Press, Chicago, 1964) is the title of this book. One wonders who is the *You?*

Such bland fare is unreal and must be unhealthy for all children, but for the black children it is positively harmful They must come away from such texts with the impression that they do not exist and perhaps do not even deserve to.

I do not believe that we can teach children anything if we deliberately ignore the facts of their world as they know them to be. My children know that blacks and whites do not very often live on the same block together; they know that cities are not clean and streets are not tree-lined. They know, because they see it every day, that children do not play together in perfect harmony, but that black children fight with white—and all children fight occasionally with each other. Nothing can be gained by pretending to the kids that this is not so.

Instead, a great deal can be learned by airing these issues and by asking children to think about and discuss the very real problems they face in school. In much the same way that children will learn to handle their own affairs if they are given the chance to try, they can only learn to cope with the social problems of their day if these are faced honestly and brought out into the open.

I thus make it a point to have my class discuss situations and problems as they come up. How very necessary this is was brought home to me in one of the very first such discussions we had. I had told the children that we would discuss the civil rights issue in social studies class next day, since we had been having some problems with the relations between white and black students in the school. They promised to think about the issue and come prepared to talk about it. Tommy started the discussion off the next day. He had carefully written up a report on the Civil War and on the Emancipation Proclamation, in which he stated that the problem of slavery had been taken care of after the Civil War, and although problems still existed in the South, the North had managed to cope with them in the American tradition of liberty and equality. He was very serious, and I could see that he was quite convinced that he was presenting an accurate and, above all, a generally acceptable picture. Sue followed suit with a report on the Bill of Rights and a discussion of what the various Rights mean. She, too, was very serious but very academic about the issue.

I looked at the black kids. They were sitting in their seats, their faces blank, silent and bored, waiting for the class to end. They had heard this many times before. It was a dangerous topic; they were withdrawn and apprehensive and wanted no part of it.

"But lets think of what goes on in our own school," I said when Sue had finished. "We can't know much about the Bill of Rights and the civil rights problem, unless we can see how it affects our own lives." Silence. The children did not know how to handle this—it was unfamiliar territory, no convenient slogans presented themselves. "Well, how do you think black and white kids get on in this school?" I persevered. "Are they friends? Do they fight? How do you think integrated education works?"

This elicited a response, but a hesitant one. The children began to move around in their seats, talk in low tones to their neighbors, whisper to their friends; did I really mean it? Should they really discuss the things that actually happened, which had not been acknowledged in the classroom before? One boy raised his hand reluctantly, "Do you mean things like what happens in the cafeteria?" he asked. "Yes, of course, things that happen in school every day," I told him. That broke the ice.

The things that happened in school every day were very important to all of them, they were all deeply involved. They began to talk about them. "Well, there are white tables and black tables," said the same boy. "I don't see why white kids and black kids can't sit together."

"But they don't like us to," cried another white boy. "I do try sometimes to join a black table, but the black kids don't want us there." "Yes, and I would be scared even to try," contributed another. Reactions were beginning to come in thick and fast. "The black boys are bullies and they would just as soon fight as not." "That is why I think that integrated schools can't work," interjected John. "At least not yet. 'They' just aren't like us—they *like* to fight." "And they take my money," added a girl. "They're always asking for money and hitting other kids." Most of the white children were involved in the discussion by now, but not a single black child had been heard from yet.

But this last remark brought Deborah to her feet to make an impassioned speech. "We don't *like* to fight, we just have to," she declared. "If you lived where I live, you would have to fight, too. And how can we be friends with you?" she wanted to know. "We come to your school, and we see how you all live here, in nice houses and with cars and everything big and nice. And then we go home and look at our living room, and it's nice and it's home and we like it, but we know how it would look like to you. And maybe you're not much yourself, but your mother is beautiful and you're proud of her, but you don't want the white kids to meet her, they might not like her so much, and besides you wouldn't even come down to the projects." Her words tumbled over themselves in her haste to get everything out. Without stopping for breath she went on, voicing all her deep feelings of mixed pride in her race and feelings of inferiority when she compared her style of living with that of her white classmates, her defiance and her envy, but above all, making us—the white people in the class—really see and feel for the first time what it must be like to be black in our school.

She had brought it all out into the open. The social problems, the great economic differences between the two worlds in school, the hollowness of the myth that "everyone is equal," the problems of race—all of it.

The class was really impressed. They had never heard a black child speak like that before; never had they been shown the deep emotions and conflicts of these "they" they talked about so glibly. They had to believe Deborah—she was so sincere, so obviously genuine. The white kids were a little ashamed now of their bland conviction that everything was for the best in the best of all possible worlds. Those who couldn't face the implications tried to gloss them over. It was so easy to find things to criticize about Deborah, things that would help discredit what she had said. She had spoken in the ghetto vernacular—I had had to stop her frequently to ask her to "translate" for us—and she made lots of mistakes when she spoke. Some picked out her shortcomings; others said no, of course, they would go to Deborah's house if they were asked, of course they would not make fun of her home and her mother, of course they could be friends. But they now had something to think about. No longer could they say easily, "The North has no problems" or "The black people are to blame for any problems that do exist." I didn't think that discussions such as these would help eradicate prejudice and bring about racial harmony, but I did feel that they would help make children face the realities of their life and begin to see the problems involved. And that is a beginning.

Discussions on the urgent issues of the day became a regular feature in my classroom. We began to think about all kinds of aspects of the black-white problem, such as the problem of violence. "Black kids are bullies," said the white boys. "Why do you think they are?" I asked. Examples abounded of black boys and girls bullying other kids, threatening to beat them up, and getting their way in that manner. "But why?" "It's natural," said the white boys. "Black people are just violent, that's all. Look at the riots in the cities."

This was too much for Deborah, who knew very well how it is to be made to feel violent. "If someone took a pen that belonged to you and wouldn't give it back no matter how often you ask for it, you would become violent too," she said, expressing the frustration of her people in a white society. "I know I would. *Anyone* can feel violent sometimes."

The boys didn't concede the point. "Look what they did to the school bus in North Carolina," said Tommy. "They just took to violence." "But Tommy," I had to intervene, "those were *white* people who overturned the bus." "It's because black people are violent," Tommy replied illogically. "Isn't that right, Dan?" he turned directly to Dan. "Don't you fight in the school bus going home? Don't you think the black kids like violence?" Dan was embarrassed and silent. (He hated these discussions and tended to avoid them. "That's not school work" he said to me when I urged him to participate. Maybe it was too painful for him—not everyone has Deborah's strength.)

But Tommy persisted.

"Isn't that true? Don't you think you people are violent? Don't you fight a lot? Don't you like violence?" His questioning was sharp and had an undertone of hostility in it, although he was pretending to be impartially and academically interested. Dan felt the hostility and his reaction was surprising: "Yes, of course we're violent," he cried, and he got up and threw out his chest, making a fist and crooking his arm. He looked at Tommy challengingly, laughing, but tense. "We love to fight, see," he was clowning now. It was as if he was saying "If that's what you want me to say, I will. Only stop prodding me, leave me alone." He was scared and confused and he wanted out. If this was his aim, he succeeded. Tommy had the wind taken out of his sails. "You see," was all he could say to the rest of the children. The discussion was over.

Debates such as these are necessarily more painful to the black kids than to the white. They must be handled with care, and when it becomes apparent that they are too painful, allowances must be made. Several times, I let Dan simply walk out of the room when I felt that he really couldn't bear to stay.

Not all discussions must be so painful. They can serve a variety of purposes. Children may become aware for instance, of their own values and of the existence of those of others. An interesting exchange developed from the question: what is democracy?

Tommy had a ready answer. "A country where everyone can make as much money as they want." Deborah gave it some thought. "A country where everyone is a human being like anyone else" was her contribution.

"How important is money, and what else is important?" This question came up when we were talking about the caste system in India. Caste decides the amount of prestige a person will have in India, we decided. "What decides it here?" The kids had to think about it. "What professions had prestige? Doctors, lawyers, senators—teachers?" "No, not teachers." "Why not, weren't they doing just as important a job as the others?" "Yes," they agreed, "but they did not make as much money." "Should money be a factor in deciding a question like that?" "Yes," the kids agreed, "it certainly should because you can't really do much without money."

The question of personal integrity came up in a discussion of the presidential campaign. "Should a politician say what he really believed in, or should he say what would get him the most votes?" This was a hard one. Only one boy was quite sure that he should say what would get him the most votes; it would be ridiculous to do anything else. Everyone else was really undecided.

If children think about such problems, they will come to grips with some of the most basic issues in human relations in our society. It is my belief that discussions such as these are as much a part of the teaching process as working with the prescribed textbooks and materials. The sooner the kids learn that there are no easy and ready-made answers to most problems, the more they learn to take a second and more profound look at things they have always taken for granted, and the better equipped they will be to deal with the complex issues of our society.

This should be part of the whole process of learning and growth that goes on in school. Children are learning all the time, in school and out, in class and on the playground, during math period and in the lunch hour. Teaching should go on all the time as well. Just as children should learn to know themselves and acquire self-control, just as they should learn to deal with others, so they must also learn to deal honestly and in a straightforward way with the intellectual problems they will have to face. But children must be allowed to act and think on their own; it does no good to "give" them opinions or present them with conclusions. They must work out the solutions themselves, otherwise they will have no meaning.

PROPOSALS AND SUGGESTIONS

How can we teach children of widely varying abilities and skills in one classroom without discouraging the less able and holding back the fast learners? This is a problem that arises in any classroom, integrated or not. In an integrated classroom, however, it is underlined by the racial issue. Closely related is the problem of discipline. Children who are made to feel frustration and failure at the academic level and who are forced to attend a class in which they cannot meaningfully participate become bored and begin to look upon themselves as worthless. They will then try to draw attention to themselves by any means they can devise. If, on the other hand, they feel some success and achievement, they will tend to concentrate more on their work. This fact again is pointed up in an integrated classroom. If teachers allow both worlds to exist and teach each to respect the other, the enforcement of true discipline will take much more time and energy than the exercise of simple control; on the other hand, it becomes imperative that as many issues as possible be dealt with in the classroom, with the participation of all children.

The only way in which we can avoid producing the "failure syndrome" is by eliminating the competitive principle from the educational system. As long as we teach to a mythical average child who is expected to possess the skills of a mythical level of learning, as long as we evaluate the performance of the individual in comparison with what randomly selected children of the same general age group are able to do, we are constantly producing unnecessary feelings of inferiority and suppressing any incentive to improve—not to mention the joy of learning. Even for usually successful children, like John, it is a painful experience when they are beaten by a rival. The situation becomes particularly tragic for black children in a school such as mine. Competing with white children of middle-class backgrounds, they tend to perceive their lack of skills—attributable to their social and economic condition—as racial, innate, and unchangeable inferiority. Unfortunately, many teachers tend to agree.

The only approach to teaching that makes any sense in human terms, it seems to me, is individualized instruction. This means that we must recognize the fact that every child learns at his own pace and in his own way. In a classroom full of children of the same age group, every student will have mastered different skills to a different degree. Every teacher who has ever conscientiously tried to teach a whole class at grade level must be all too familiar with what happens.

Consider, for example, a fifth-grade math class. I begin to teach multiplication. Immediately, I have two groups: those students who know how to multiply, and those who do not. When I begin to pay attention to the ones who do, I acquire two more groups: those who know how to multiply with one number, and those who know how to multiply with two. I then turn my attention to those who cannot multiply at all: they, too, fall into several groups: those who do not know the multiplication tables, those who know the tables but do not know how to add properly, and those who know how to do both these operations, but cannot remember the sequence and procedure. The closer the attention I pay to each of these groups, the more different groups emerge. Inevitably, I end up with a class of individuals, each one with a particular problem. Unfortunately, the teacher is only one person; it is impossible for him to handle all of these problems by himself.

One solution, in my view, is programmed instruction. Many such programs are available today; it is only necessary for the school to acquire several different kinds, so that the teacher can select the one most appropriate for his particular group.

I personally have had the greatest success with a math program—math being a subject that is comparatively easy to break down into different levels and sequential steps. IPI (Individualized Prescribed Instruction), I have found, is appliable to any elementary group. This program first diagnoses a student's skill deficiencies and then prescribes the specific work to be done, in carefully graded steps. The child must make sure that he has the skills at one level before proceeding to the next.

My experience with this program has been that children are anxious to work in it. Once the diagnosis is made, the student can work on his own. He feels, as he proceeds, that he is being successful and is making visible progress. Admittedly, children will realize that some are working at more advanced levels than they themselves are. This is only natural and inevitable. But a realization that some are more skilled than others is quite different from saying, "*All* should know this, and those who don't are behind." Never, under this system, are children forced to publicly acknowledge and expose their "inferiority" to a group. Neither are they ever pilloried for their weaknesses. Instead, we give them a sense of security by showing them exactly why they are weak in a certain area and what they can do about it. It is one thing to be asked for an answer in front of the entire class and have to admit that one doesn't know it; it is quite another to tell a child, "If you want to do *this,* you will have to learn *this* first, and this is the way you can go about it." There will be great satisfaction for every child in proceeding from one step to the next, in seeing unmistakable signs of achievement.

In an integrated class, a program such as this has added advantages. The diagnosis clearly shows the great diversity of skills that exists in one class. This helps to explode the theory that it is only the black kids who are "dumb." It helps black children, discouraged by the fact that they are constantly being asked to perform tasks they are unable to do, by letting them experience success. Finally, this kind of program is highly structured. The constant reassurance that they are doing the right thing, which children like Ruthie and Greg so desperately need, is built into the system. At every step they can check whether they are doing well and they are allowed to try again until they do.

Helpful as it may be, a program such as IPI should be used with the full realization of what it *cannot* do. It can and does help children acquire mechanical skills, but it cannot provide a substitute for the human relations aspect of the classroom. If an answer book can provide reassurance, this does not mean that human reassurance, approval, and warmth from the teacher become unnecessary. Neither should instruction be individualized to the point where group dynamics become unimportant. It is interesting to note that even the children who are most enthusiastic about the IPI program in my class miss the group work to which they have become accustomed. No program can eliminate the need for interaction between the children; it is true, however, that once children are freed from the necessity to compete with each other by artificially set standards, they will seek out those of their classmates with whom they can most comfortably work—interaction then becomes much more effective.

There are other areas where the program cannot be relied on. Such skills as making judgments and interpretations, and growth processes such as learning self-direction and taking on responsibility cannot be taught by a machine.

It is not always necessary, however, to rely on a formalized program such as IPI. It is quite possible, I found, to make up individualized programs of your own, programs that combine the teaching of mechanical skills with the other learning that should go on in the classroom.

Take my spelling program, for example. I found the spelling books used in the school quite unsuitable for my purposes. To me, there seemed very little sense in giving all children the same set of words to learn, regardless of whether they had any use for them or not. I decided, instead, to let the children make up their own spelling lists. They are required to read one book every two weeks. They may select from the library any book that interests them; once a week they must submit a list of spelling words culled from their reading and prove to me that they know how to use them. Words come alive in the most surprising ways. One boy who became annoyed with me during the spelling period, seized the opportunity to hurl two of his brand new words at me, "You," he cried, "are an impudent ignoramus!"

The program has worked out very well. Participants like this way of learning how to spell and work hard at it. For the slower readers, the program acts as an incentive. Only those who have finished work on the basic words they will have to use every day are allowed to join. They work hard to improve their spelling, so eager are they to be allowed into the program.

The program is structured so that children will learn more than just spelling. Every student is responsible for his own reading and for his word lists. He is on his honor to produce a new list every week and he is expected to be disciplined enough to do the work on his own. Occasionally, a student will try to cheat and use the same list for several weeks. When discovered, this can provide an excellent opportunity for teaching self-reliance and self-discipline. Finally, children work in teams of two and correct each other's papers. In this way, I hope, my students will learn to work together and help each other—another important part of the learning that goes on in school.

It must be obvious that individualized instruction—whatever the form it may take—puts a far greater burden on the teacher than he has to carry in the traditional system. It is difficult, if not impossible, for one person to do this alone.

The problem of the need for more help in the classroom could be solved in a variety of ways. One is the use of volunteers. The White Plains school system employs a coordinator of volunteers who makes help available to any teacher who asks for it. Volunteers can be used in many subject areas and in different ways. They can—as was done with Ted—take a child with a particular difficulty and work with him on a one-to-one basis outside of the classroom. This not only helps the child but also frees the teacher to deal with the other students. In addition, it may help to prevent some behavior problems. Dick, for example, who acted up in class because he could not participate, became warmly attached to one of the volunteers and enjoyed at least a part of his school day.

Volunteers can also be used with groups of children. If a teacher feels that some children need more of his attention than others, he can divide his class for certain periods of the day and direct a volunteer how to take care of the group that can work on its own, while he helps the other.

It is not only the child who is behind who needs special attention. Volunteers with special skills should be used to provide the enrichment needed by students with unusual interests. I had a very good experience with two high school students: one came to school one afternoon a week, after school hours, and took a group of students who were especially interested in math. He did such a good job that the children were eager for him to come, although it meant staying after school. The other one was a graduate of the high school black studies program. He came to tell the children about the black experience in America and he, too, made a tremendous impression.

Volunteers should be recruited from a variety of sources. One such source could be neighboring teacher training institutions. They might encourage their freshmen to work in the schools as part of their academic credit. Future teachers could then find out at an early stage in their training whether or not this is really the profession for them.

If we decide to teach the individual, we must also evaluate the individual and his effort and progress, rather than comparing students' achievements with those of their peers. As it now stands the system of evaluation in my school requires that the teacher grade every child in relation to his class. This means that even if a child has exerted tremendous effort and made great progress, he may *have* to be given a bad grade, if his standing is poor compared with others in the class. The fact that this system of evaluation is harmful, especially in an integrated classroom, has been recognized by the Board of Education and was pointed out by the superintendent of schools in his 1967 report on the racial balance plan:

> Another dilemma was presented by grading and reporting procedures. Certain disadvantaged pupils made evident progress within the marking period, yet still lagged some distance behind the achievement of more privileged youngsters. The question naturally arose: how can you give grades that reward and encourage disadvantaged children without being unfair to youngsters who achieve at a level well above average?

A committee of teachers is now at work on a recommendation to revise the grading system.

I believe strongly that the problem of being unfair to anyone would not arise if we gave up the system of comparative grading. All children should be evaluated in relation to their own effort and their own achievement. Reports to parents should reflect a child's particular strengths and weaknesses, both academic and nonacademic. The present system leaves no room for comment on special talents not directly related to the skills needed in school. One of my brightest students one year had an extraordinary aptitude for making satiric cartoons. This shows a great ability to analyze, identify salient points, make judgments, and express a conclusion in a highly condensed and sophisticated way, yet the framework of the report cards did not allow me to mention it! Such reports should also outline a child's general development and his human growth—he lacks a sense of responsibility, he is too dependent on the opinion of his peers, he has made great strides in self-control—all such comments are useful for the parents to know and vitally important for the child.

Record cards on students, which are for the use of their future teachers, should contain checklists of skills he has and of those he lacks, so that every teacher with a new class will know where to begin with every individual. Grades, as they are awarded now, are nebulous, imprecise, and have little meaning to a teacher who did not award them.

An individualized approach to teaching can go far towards solving the problems raised by integrating two different worlds into one classroom. The same principle must be applied in dealing with behavior problems that come up. As far as possible, the teacher must try to see why every child behaves in a particular way and deal with him accordingly. As far as possible, every child must be taught self-control and respect for others. In an integrated classroom, it is doubly important to deal successfully with behavior problems; failure in this respect with the black children can too easily lead to a reinforcement of prejudice.

If every child is to be treated as an individual, and if all problems are to be dealt with consistently and patiently, the teacher will need help in these areas also. Charged with the care of a class of 25 to 28 children, he cannot possibly establish the kind of discipline in which I believe and take the time to handle each situation as it comes up.

I would thus like to see the establishment of a new position in the elementary schools: a full-time counselor, who would be responsible for both long-term and emergency situations. Such a person would not necessarily have to have special training; it could be any teacher who has particular ability in handling difficult children. He could work with individuals or with small groups and would take over children who, for one reason or another, cannot be kept in a classroom without doing harm to themselves and to the other students. Instead of sending such children to the office or out into the halls, making them feel invisible and worthless, the teacher could refer such children to the counselor, who would deal with their problems constructively.

The counselor, however, should not serve as an excuse for the teacher and the students not to deal with each other. Only in situations where a child cannot be kept in the classroom should the counselor be called in. In other cases he might take over a teacher's class for a short period, while the teacher handles a problem for which he needs additional time.

As he comes to know the school and the children, the counselor could become a resource person, advising all teachers on how to handle certain problems. He would also be a useful source of information for the social workers, psychologists, and home-school counselors, who spend only a part of their time in each school and cannot usually see the problems that arise in their full context.

Several steps could be taken to improve communication between the school and the parents, black and white alike. These can be strictly practical—the principal of my school, for example, has submitted a request for funds to provide transportation for black parents to the school whenever they may need it—or the school and parents can try to tackle profounder problems.

It might be a good idea to hold regular human relations workshops for parents in every class. The workshops should be led by persons who are familiar with the problems of the school—the counselor if there is one, or the home-school counselors. These workshops would discuss the special problems that come up in the class. Organized on the principle of sensitivity training groups, the workshops could discuss the problems that come up between the races, complaints on teacher prejudice, or bullying of white children by black, or an issue such as the race that had to be run over again. Misunderstandings and disputes could be openly aired and talked about honestly in an effort to increase understanding between parents, teachers, and children.

It cannot be too strongly emphasized that all the problems discussed here are those that come up regularly and frequently in any classroom; the solutions proposed are valid for any school. None of the proposals voiced here are aimed solely at the problem of integration. It seems to me, however, that an integrated classroom serves to point up the urgency of many of these questions, perhaps because the racial issue is so intimately tied up with most of our human and social problems.

TOWARDS INTEGRATION

In 1968, three years after the racial balance plan was implemented, the then superintendent of schools in White Plains, Carroll F. Johnson, published an evaluation of the results ("Achieving Racial Balance," *School Management Magazine*, January 1968). According to a study done by the White Plains Board of Education, none of the objections and fears voiced about the plan prior to its implementation had come true.

White children in the newly integrated schools had suffered no setback. According to tests made this group continued to perform either at the same level as before 1964, or slightly above. More black children were making greater progress than comparable groups of center-city children before the plan went into effect.

Questionnaires had been submitted to both parents and teachers, asking for their reactions to the plan. Results indicated that a majority of the parents either saw only positive effects or thought that integration had made no difference one way or the other. Only a minority could see only negative effects. A majority, 56.5, per cent of the elementary teachers who responded felt that the plan had both positive and negative aspects, while 29 per cent saw only positive results, and 9.7 per cent saw only negative aspects.

The conclusion that the community was increasingly accepting the plan was bolstered by the fact that there had been no large-scale flight of middle-class families from the public schools. Although, admittedly, the study was of a limited nature, the board and the superintendent declared themselves very satisfied with the success of the plan.

The plan's most determined opponents, the Committee on Schools, made its own study. Even it had to concede that white children had not suffered from the integration program, but it maintained, however, that black students did perform at a "significantly low level of achievement."

An investigation by an independent agency does not agree. In a simultaneous study, the Center for Urban Education agrees, though somewhat cautiously, with the conclusion of the superintendent and the Board of Education. Its evaluation is summed up in these words:

> Summary: the main objective of the Racial Balance Plan has been accomplished. The proportion of Negro children in each school has been stabilized within the intended guidelines. [by 1970, a re-distribution of Negro children among the several schools had to be undertaken, because of changing housing patterns]. Positive responses to the Plan—by parents (white and Negro), teachers and administrators—outweigh negative responses, the high academic level of achievement of white students has not been adversely affected. Thus far, the achievements of center city children who entered balanced schools no earlier than third grade has not been markedly improved; however, there is slight evidence of some success with center city children who entered balanced schools at first grade. (Arley Bondarin, *The Racial Balance Plan*, Center for Urban Education, publication No. PRS 001, p. 26).

On balance then, the conclusion is that the plan has been a qualified success. None of the arguments against it have proven to be valid. All sources agree that white parents have nothing to fear from integration, although there is disagreement on the effect on the academic achievement of black children.

This is welcome news. I submit, however, that we have

taken only a first step. We have not yet succeeded in integrating our elementary schools; all we have achieved is desegregation. A long and difficult road lies ahead.

Most of these studies concentrated on levels of academic achievement; I would like to stress the human factor. It is in the elementary schools, I feel, that real integration should be attempted. Contact in the elementary classroom is close and constant; children remain in one group and work with one another throughout the school day. True understanding can come only through *living* together. Children, if left to interact freely, will come to know each other and will learn to acknowledge and accept the existence of standards and mores different from their own. Vague ideals, nebulous fears, and blissful ignorance all can be dispelled in an honest attempt to see reality and deal with it. It is then that we can tackle the task of closing the skills gap, which does so much to separate the races on the intermediate and secondary levels of the school system.

Integration must be a two-way street. It may be impossible to do cross-busing today; to make it possible tomorrow, it is imperative that we establish a two-way communication in the classroom at as early an age as possible. Both sides must learn to accept, respect, and understand the other.

In the classroom, integration should mean a truly equal opportunity for every child. The student who works hard and succeeds, the one who does not work at all, the one who is quiet and well behaved, and the one who disrupts the class, all are telling us something, all must be heard. Every child must be given the opportunity to *be*—to be *himself,* not what someone else thinks he *should* be. Every child must have an opportunity to learn in his own way and an opportunity to grow and mature and understand. All this must take place in the classroom every day. If integration is to succeed, it must become the personal concern of every individual in the school. Teachers and students, parents and administrators, all must work on themselves—for adults, too, must gain in self-knowledge, self-discipline, and understanding—and with each other if we are to achieve our goal.

"To integrate," according to the dictionary, is "to become united so as to form a complete or perfect whole." I believe that we can not become a complete or perfect whole unless and until we first allow every individual and every group their right to a separate existence.